My
Windows® 8.1

Katherine Murray

que®

800 East 96th Street
Indianapolis, Indiana 46240 USA

My Windows® 8.1

Copyright © 2014 by Pearson Education, Inc.

ISBN-13: 978-0-7897-5222-2
ISBN-10: 0-7897-5222-0

Library of Congress Cataloging-in-Publication Data is on file.

Printed in the United States of America

First Printing: October 2013

Trademarks

All terms mentioned in this book that are known to be trademarks or service marks have been appropriately capitalized. Que Publishing cannot attest to the accuracy of this information. Use of a term in this book should not be regarded as affecting the validity of any trademark or service mark.

Windows is a registered trademark of Microsoft Corporation.

Warning and Disclaimer

Every effort has been made to make this book as complete and as accurate as possible, but no warranty or fitness is implied. The information provided is on an "as is" basis. The author and the publisher shall have neither liability nor responsibility to any person or entity with respect to any loss or damages arising from the information contained in this book.

Bulk Sales

Que Publishing offers excellent discounts on this book when ordered in quantity for bulk purchases or special sales. For more information, please contact

U.S. Corporate and Government Sales

1-800-382-3419

corpsales@pearsontechgroup.com

For sales outside of the U.S., please contact

International Sales

international@pearsoned.com

Editor-in-Chief
Greg Wiegand

Executive Editor
Loretta Yates

Development Editor
Brandon Cackowski-Schnell

Managing Editor
Sandra Schroeder

Senior Project Editor
Tonya Simpson

Copy Editor
Megan Wade-Taxter

Senior Indexer
Cheryl Lenser

Proofreader
Sarah Kearns

Technical Editor
Laura Acklen

Editorial Assistant
Cindy Teeters

Interior Designer
Anne Jones

Cover Designer
Mark Shirar

Compositor
Mary Sudul

Contents at a Glance

Table of Contents

3   Using and Tweaking the Start Screen   61

8   Organizing Files with File Explorer   179

About the Author

After writing about technology for more than 25 years, **Katherine Murray** believes there's never been a better time to be a tech enthusiast. She has seen personal computing change from big, slow, cryptic desktop-hogging machines to small, sleek smart devices we can tap our way through easily. She has worked with every version of Microsoft Windows there's been, loving some versions (such as Windows 7) and loathing others (remember Windows Vista?). But now with Windows 8.1, she feels Microsoft is in sync with the times, offering a fast, fluid, and secure option for connecting with others, enjoying media, saving to the cloud, and integrating our work across multiple devices. She started writing about technology 25 years ago and still enjoys it, specializing in Microsoft technologies and the fascinating ways in which we stay in touch with each other. In addition to writing books, she writes regularly for *Windows Secrets* magazine.

Dedication

This book is for you if you love color and movement and like your technology to behave. I hope you enjoy Windows 8.1!

Acknowledgments

Another great project with the Que team! My thanks to the team at Que Publishing, for their hard work and quick-but-doable schedules. Special thanks to Loretta Yates, as always, for being so great to work with; to Brandon Cackowski-Schnell, development editor, for all his help along the way; to Laura Acklen, technical editor, for her good catches and friendly suggestions; to Megan Wade-Taxter, for a fine and careful copy edit; and to Tonya Simpson, project editor, for shepherding this book through the production process.

We Want to Hear from You!

As the reader of this book, *you* are our most important critic and commentator. We value your opinion and want to know what we're doing right, what we could do better, what areas you'd like to see us publish in, and any other words of wisdom you're willing to pass our way.

We welcome your comments. You can email or write to let us know what you did or didn't like about this book—as well as what we can do to make our books better.

Please note that we cannot help you with technical problems related to the topic of this book.

When you write, please be sure to include this book's title and author as well as your name and email address. We will carefully review your comments and share them with the author and editors who worked on the book.

Email: feedback@quepublishing.com

Mail: Que Publishing
ATTN: Reader Feedback
800 East 96th Street
Indianapolis, IN 46240 USA

Reader Services

Visit our website and register this book at quepublishing.com/register for convenient access to any updates, downloads, or errata that might be available for this book.

Introduction

When Microsoft unveiled Windows 8, some people were pleased, and some weren't. Those who were eager to use Windows on their tablets and other touch devices seemed to get behind the new features fairly quickly and enjoyed the new experience. Those who weren't convinced they *needed* a new operating system—or who were still very happy with Windows 7, thank you very much—lamented the big changes Windows 8 brought and quickly began crying "foul."

As Microsoft is known to do (sometimes later rather than sooner), they listened to their critics and offered, in Windows 8.1, a way to stay the course of their vision while doing a better job supporting those who had misgivings about such a big change. For those who were mourning the loss of the Start menu, a new Windows 8 Start button appeared. For folks who had a problem with the big split between the look and function of the Windows 8 Start screen and the Windows 8 Desktop, Microsoft added the ability to use the same background for both features. For those who were reasonably happy with the first blush of Windows 8, all sorts of new enhancements began to emerge, ranging from improvements in PC Settings to new touch gestures to a makeover of the Windows Store and the Music app, just to name a few.

Windows 8.1 is more than a slight upgrade to Microsoft's first ambitious effort at totally revamping the way we use technology today. It includes improvements to the basic tasks we want our operating system to perform and adds many enhancements and capabilities to make finding, sharing, and enjoying media and more easier than ever.

Throughout this book, you'll learn about and work with the variety of new features available in Windows 8.1 and find out how to enhance and personalize the operating system so that it does what you want it to do—smoothly.

Versions of Windows 8.1

Microsoft is offering Windows 8.1 as a free upgrade for each of the three versions of Windows 8 currently in use:

- **Windows 8.1 (32-bit and 64-bit)**—The standard version used by the majority of individual computer users. You can upgrade to Windows 8.1 free of charge on your Windows 8 system by downloading it from the Windows Store or ordering it on DVD. Your applications, Windows settings, and files will be intact after the upgrade.

- **Windows 8.1 Pro (also in 32-bit and 64-bit versions)**—The upgrade for Windows 8 Pro, which adds high-end features like BitLocker, Client Hyper-V, and (in some editions) Windows Media Center. You can upgrade from the Windows Store or by ordering media for installation.

- **Windows RT 8.1**—The upgrade for Windows RT, which is the version of Windows available for tablets that run on Acorn RISC Machine (ARM) processors. This version of Windows contains a slightly different feature set and is available only when you purchase a new ARM tablet, so it comes preinstalled on the equipment for you. You can upgrade to Windows RT 8.1 only through the Windows Store.

Microsoft also sells Windows 8—and now, Windows 8.1—by volume licensing in Windows 8.1 and Windows 8.1 Enterprise versions. The upgrade to Windows 8.1 Enterprise is available by media only from Windows 8 Pro, Windows 8 Pro with Media Center, and Windows 8 Enterprise.

WHAT'S ARM?

Windows RT 8.1 is for tablets and devices running on ARM processors. These processors are used in many mobile devices today, offering a simple design that works well in low-power situations. The Android smartphone and tablet are two examples of hugely popular devices running on ARM.

Microsoft released Windows RT for devices running on ARM architecture because this move extends the reach of Windows into a huge market segment. Because Windows 8.1 is designed for touch, Microsoft needs to ensure that Windows 8.1 can be used on as many different touch-enabled devices as possible. With so many devices today running on ARM processors, Microsoft needed to address this ARM space to be a serious contender in the mobile market. Windows RT 8.1 also includes touch-capable versions of Microsoft Office, which is a big perk not included with the standard Windows 8.1 or Windows 8.1 Pro. The examples in this book use Windows 8.1 to demonstrate the play-by-play for the various tasks you'll want to try.

Highlights of Windows 8.1

Some of the features in Windows 8.1 are designed to quiet the critics of the original Windows 8, but the majority of what you'll find in Windows 8.1 are improvements to the overall system. You'll find a wide range of personalization options that will help you create the Windows 8.1 experience you're comfortable with. You'll also find ways to change how you find, install, display, and work with your apps and learn about the new and enhanced apps included with Windows 8.1. Here's a quick list of some of the major changes and additions you'll discover:

- The return of the Start button on the Windows 8.1 Desktop enables you to move back and forth between the Start screen and Desktop easily. You can also display a menu with a simple right-click.

- Now you can boot Windows 8.1 directly to the Desktop and bypass the Start screen altogether.

- You can customize the Start screen by adding your own backgrounds and choosing animations.

- You can change the size of app tiles (Windows 8.1 includes new sizes) and choose the way you want them to appear by default.

- You can use new touch gestures and additional onscreen keyboard features to navigate and input information more easily than ever.

- You can watch a live slideshow on your Lock Screen and receive updates and make calls without unlocking your computer.

- You can customize the Desktop with your own photos (you can use the same background picture for the Start screen if you like).

- You can move files to and from SkyDrive more easily with the enhanced integration in Windows 8.1.

- You can use the new Help and Tips app to learn the basics of Windows 8.1 and watch a tutorial about new features and tasks.

- You can discover and download new apps in the revamped Windows Store, try the new apps included with Windows 8.1, create playlists and organize your music with the updated Music app, and edit your photos and apply filters and more with the enhanced Photos app.

- You can explore the new PC Settings (and move away from the Control Panel for most settings).

- You can browse with the new Internet Explorer 11 and experience improvements with tabbed browsing.

>>>Go Further

THERE'S TOUCH—AND THEN THERE'S WINDOWS 8.1 TOUCH

Windows 8.1 runs on any computer that previously ran Windows 8 or Windows 7, which means you can use a number of touch-capable devices with Windows 8.1 (and new devices are coming). When you install Windows 8.1, the operating system does a quick check of your hardware to see whether it can make use of the new touch sensitivities in Windows 8. If your computer is a non-Windows 8.1 computer or device (you might be upgrading to Windows 8.1 on a system that previously ran Windows 7, for example), you might see a message that your system isn't optimized for Windows 8.1 touch. Don't worry—touch will still work. Microsoft is simply telling you that your touchscreen might not be as wonderfully responsive as it would be if you had hardware designed specifically for Windows 8.1. (Cue the Microsoft Surface commercial.)

If you are using an ARM tablet with Windows RT, you might not notice anything missing in your machine's touch capabilities. But if you put the non-Windows 8.1 tablet up against one designed to run optimally with Windows 8.1, you will notice a greater precision in the way the system picks up gestures, as well as a larger area of the screen where it is most receptive to touch. (Windows 8.1 surfaces were designed so that the device is touch-capable all the way out to the edge of the screen.)

What You'll Find in This Book

In this book, you'll discover what you need to know to accomplish all the basic tasks you want to do with Windows 8.1. We'll focus first on the features you're most likely to want to know upfront; then we explore some of the more specialized tasks, such as working with File Explorer, navigating Internet Explorer 11, and unboxing all the apps. The chapters unfold like this:

- Chapter 1, "First Look at Windows 8.1," gets you started with the basics of Windows 8.1 and gives you a view of the new operating system. You'll learn how to use touch gestures, as well as the mouse and keyboard, to navigate with Windows 8.1. You'll also find out how to put Windows 8.1 to sleep, wake it up, and power down your computer.

- Chapter 2, "Preparing Your PC and Setting Up Devices," shows you how to set up devices so that you can use them with Windows 8.1. You'll also set app notifications, make sure you have Internet access, learn about managing your PC's power, and find out how to refresh or reset your system.

- Chapter 3, "Using and Tweaking the Start Screen," shows you how to navigate the new interface in Windows 8.1. You'll learn how to organize app tiles the way you want them, navigate in the way that fits you best, show more tiles on the Start screen, and tweak settings so that the Start screen launches you right into the tasks you most want to accomplish with Windows 8.1.

- Chapter 4, "Working with the Desktop," introduces you to the new Start button and shows you how to boot directly to the Desktop. You'll also learn how to launch and work with programs on the Desktop and tailor the taskbar to include the Quick Launch items you want.

- Chapter 5, "Making It Your Windows 8.1," covers all kinds of personalization features, beginning with customizations for the Lock screen, color schemes, profile picture, badges, notifications, and accessibility features.

- Chapter 6, "Securing Your Computer," helps you ensure that your computer is as safe as possible by setting a password, customizing your login, creating user accounts, adding a PIN logon, setting location privacy, and telling Windows 8.1 how—or whether—you want apps to share your information.

- Chapter 7, "Diving In with Apps," introduces you to the new Windows Store and shows you how to find, download, install, and update the apps that interest you. You'll also learn how to work with multiple apps on the screen at once, use Snap to arrange them on the screen, and move among open apps.

- Chapter 8, "Organizing Files with File Explorer," spotlights the tasks you need to know to organize your files and folders in Windows 8.1. Along the way, you'll learn to manage the changes in File Explorer and discover how easily you can copy, move, and share your files with others.

- Chapter 9, "Browsing with Internet Explorer 11," showcases the latest version of Microsoft's popular web browser, including the dramatically improved tabbed browsing. You'll learn how to find and manage content, save and choose favorites, and check your security settings.

- Chapter 10, "Connect and Communicate with Windows 8.1," walks you through the dramatic makeover of the Mail app and helps you set up and stay in touch with your friends and family through social media. You'll also learn about the Calendar app and find out how to use Skype to send instant messages to those on your contacts list.

- Chapter 11, "Media and More," takes a close look at the sweeping changes in the Photos app, exploring the new editing features and filters. You'll also learn about the improvements in the Music app and discover how to stream movies on your Windows 8.1 computer or device and share media and games on your Xbox.

- Chapter 12, "Working in the Cloud," explores the deep SkyDrive Integration throughout Windows 8.1. You'll learn how to set up your SkyDrive account, connect multiple accounts, work seamlessly with Office Web Apps and Office 365, and share files and coauthor in real time in the cloud. Also in this chapter, you'll learn how you can share files among all the PCs and devices in your home.

- Chapter 13, "Feeding and Troubleshooting Your PC," gives you some basic pointers on how to regularly back up your files, update your copy of Windows, and use Windows 8.1 system tools to improve your computer's performance and clean up your hard drive.

- Finally, Appendix A, "Windows 8.1 App Gallery," spotlights a collection of new apps in the Windows Store. You get a look at some popular apps and find out how to search and add to the Store on your own.

The chapters are organized so that you can jump in and read about whatever interests you most, or you can choose to go through the book sequentially if you like. Along the way, you'll find tips, notes, and two kinds of sidebars: Go Further, which gives you additional information about getting more from the topic at hand, and It's Not All Good, which lists common pitfalls and trouble spots to watch out for.

Let's Begin

Because Windows 8.1 is an upgrade, you'll most likely upgrade either by going to the Windows Store and downloading and installing Windows 8.1 or by ordering media (so the software arrives on DVD).

Either way, be sure to back up important files on your computer before you install Windows 8.1. Microsoft also suggests that you make a recovery disk so you can return your computer to normal if a hiccup happens.

After the upgrade is complete (it takes just a few minutes), your computer will restart and you'll see the Windows 8.1 Lock screen. That's where we'll begin exploring Windows 8.1 together.

The new Windows 8.1
Start screen design is
more flexible, colorful, and
customizable than ever

You can easily display
thumbnails of all the
apps you have open

In this chapter, you learn how to get started with Windows 8.1 and use touch, mouse, and keyboard to perform tasks such as

→ Discovering Windows 8.1

→ Using touch in Windows 8.1

→ Getting around with the mouse and keyboard

→ Shutting down or putting Windows to sleep

→ Finding the help you need

First Look at Windows 8.1

Whether you've been using Windows 8 for a while or you're just considering upgrading now that Windows 8.1 is on the loose, you might feel you have a lot to learn about the new operating system from Microsoft. After all, Windows 8—and now, Windows 8.1—dramatically changes the way we use our computers. Gone are menus of options and dialog boxes full of choices we can click. The Windows 8.1 Start screen offers us lots of information, color, and movement in a tappable, clickable, or swipable display.

How will you find what you need so you can actually be productive with—and maybe even enjoy using—this new release?

That's precisely the question this book is here to help you answer. You'll learn the basics of Windows 8.1 in a way that helps you keep your stress level low and your productivity level high. I liked Windows 8 right off the bat, even though many folks resisted it and criticized the sweeping new design. I loved the color and the flexibility of the new release, and I think Windows 8.1 makes improvements where they were needed and gives us further options for personalizing our Windows experience. It's all good.

This chapter introduces you to Windows 8.1 and gives you a chance to navigate the operating system using touch, mouse, and keyboard.

You'll also find out how to put your computer to sleep (no singing required) and power down the system completely, when you're ready to do that.

Introducing Windows 8.1

If you've just upgraded to Windows 8.1, the utility will restart your computer after installation is complete. When your computer restarts, Windows 8.1 quickly appears on your screen and walks you through a series of Express Setup questions (which help the operating system get you connected to the Internet, set your sharing preferences, and turn on the Do Not Track setting in Internet Explorer). One of those questions asks you whether you plan to use a SkyDrive account. (Rumor has it that SkyDrive might be renamed in the future, but as of this writing, it's still SkyDrive.) If you answer yes, Express Setup connects your computer to SkyDrive so that you're ready to use the cloud right off the bat. After you answer all the necessary questions, Windows 8.1 lets you know that you are ready to begin.

If you're powering up a new Windows 8.1 computer for the first time, the operating system launches and asks you those same Express Setup questions. Just respond as prompted and soon you'll be looking at the beautiful Windows 8.1 Start screen along with the rest of us.

A First Look!

As the operating system for your computer, Windows 8.1 tells your hardware how to interact with the software you want to use. That means that as soon as you press the power button to start your PC or touch device, Windows 8.1 launches and begins doing its work. Here are the simple steps for starting your computer and displaying the Windows 8.1 Start screen:

1. Press the Power button on your PC or device. Your Windows 8.1 Lock screen appears.
2. Swipe up on the screen (if you have a touch-capable computer), or press any key to display your login information.
3. Enter your password and either press Enter or click the arrow.
4. Now you're ready to review the various elements on the Windows 8.1 Start screen.

Additional Sign-in Choices

You can click the Sign-In Options link below the Password field if you want to see alternative ways of logging in to Windows 8.1. The first selection enables you to enter a PIN you have previously created (I'll show you how to do that in Chapter 6); the second option, which is selected by default, signs you in using your Microsoft Account.

Touring the Start Screen

Windows 8 didn't lack anything in the color department, and Windows 8.1 follows that vibrant beginning by offering an even greater number of color schemes, patterns, and personalizations. You can set up the screen to be as full of color, detail, and apps as you choose—or as minimal as you desire. When you first fire up Windows 8.1, the Start screen is pretty simple: a blue background with lighter blue accents and big app tiles that are easy to read. But after you blink a few times and get used to the color, you'll likely want to know how to do what you need to do with Windows 8.1. Here are some of the big features in Windows 8.1, which you'll find described in more detail throughout this book:

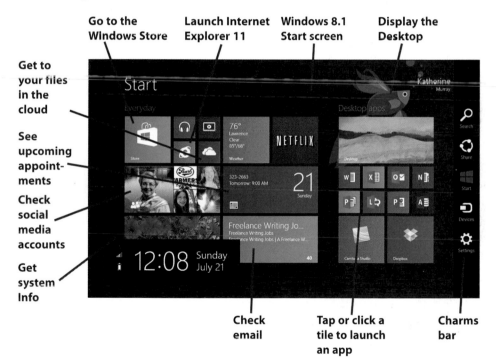

Go to the Windows Store · Launch Internet Explorer 11 · Windows 8.1 Start screen · Display the Desktop · Get to your files in the cloud · See upcoming appointments · Check social media accounts · Get system Info · Check email · Tap or click a tile to launch an app · Charms bar

- **Use the Windows 8.1 Start screen**—The Start screen can serve as the central point from where you get lots of information about friends, colleagues, weather, email, and more. Or, now in Windows 8.1, you can launch straight to the desktop if you prefer. But if you like the look and feel of the Start screen as I do, you'll find it offers you an enormous amount of information in Windows 8.1. You can see at a glance the number of email messages you have, what your day's appointments look like, what the news headlines are, and much more. Plus you can start your favorite apps, play media, change system settings, and even customize the look of Windows 8.1, all from this one screen. You'll learn more about the Start screen in Chapter 3, "Using and Tweaking the Start Screen," and find out how to personalize your Start screen in Chapter 5, "Making It *Your* Windows 8.1."

Giving the Desktop and the Start Screen the Same Look
Now you can use your Desktop background as the same background you see for your Windows 8.1 Start screen. Find out how in Chapter 5.

- **Go to your Desktop**—The Windows 8.1 Desktop will look familiar to you if you've used previous versions of Windows. Here you'll work with programs designed for Windows versions prior to Windows 8.1 (known as *legacy* programs). You find out how to use and personalize the Windows 8.1 desktop in Chapter 4, "Working with the Desktop."

- **Launch and work with apps**—The colorful tiles on the Windows 8.1 Start screen represent apps, or programs, you can launch with a simple click or tap. Some apps display "live" information and update on the Start screen, and others don't. You learn how to work with, organize, and get new apps in Chapter 7, "Diving In with Apps." Also be sure to check out the Apps Gallery in this book's appendix to find out more about the apps included with Windows 8.1 as well as popular apps in the Windows Store.

Arrange Apps Your Way
Now in Windows 8.1, it's easier than ever to group and work with clusters of apps. You learn how to do this in Chapter 3.

- **Browse the Web with Internet Explorer 11**—Internet Explorer (IE) 11 is the newest version of Microsoft's web browser, and in Windows 8.1 the big changes are that it now supports active tabs (similar to Firefox and Chrome browsers). Similar to IE 10, the web browser comes as what Microsoft calls a "modern" browser without the traditional browser window or navigation tools taking up space on the screen and a desktop version that looks more like your traditional Microsoft browser. You don't have to worry about which flavor of browser you use; the program switches automatically based on the content of the site and what you're trying to do there. You find out more about using Internet Explorer 11 in Chapter 9.

- **View, organize, and share photos**—The Photos app in Windows 8.1 has some great new features that not only make it simple to view, organize, and share all the photos you take, no matter where they're stored, but also lets you edit your photos and apply special effects and filters to add an artistic touch. You'll learn more about managing your photos in Chapter 11, "Media and More."

- **Stay up to date with friends and family**—The People app pulls together your favorite social media contacts and displays updates in live feeds that you can use to stay in sync with what your favorite folks are posting. You'll learn more about using the People app, email, and other communication tools in Chapter 10, "Connect and Communicate with Windows 8.1."

- **Find new favorites in the Windows Store**—The Windows Store is greatly improved in Windows 8.1, with a dramatic redesign from the Windows 8 version and thousands of new apps, ready for downloading. The Windows Store is where you can find apps of all sorts, free and otherwise. You'll find out more about browsing and shopping in the Windows Store in Chapter 7. You'll also get additional information about the Windows Store in the appendix of this book.

- **Work with the Charms**—A simple swipe in from the right side of the screen (or moving the mouse to the upper- or lower-right corner of the screen) displays the Charms bar, where you'll find the tools you need for searching for files, apps, and settings; sharing content and apps; returning to the Start screen; connecting devices; and changing system settings. You'll learn more about using the Charms throughout the book in the chapters related to their function.

- **Use Windows 8.1 your way**—In Windows 8.1, Microsoft made the All Apps view easier to display so that you can see all the apps you have installed without having to scroll to the right to find just the tile you need on the Start screen. You can display All Apps view by swiping up on the Start screen or by clicking the down arrow that appears when you move the mouse to the bottom of the screen. All Apps view initially shows your apps organized alphabetically by name, but you can categorize and reorder the apps to make them easier to find. You'll learn how to do that in Chapter 3.

All Apps view

Swipe up
to display
the view

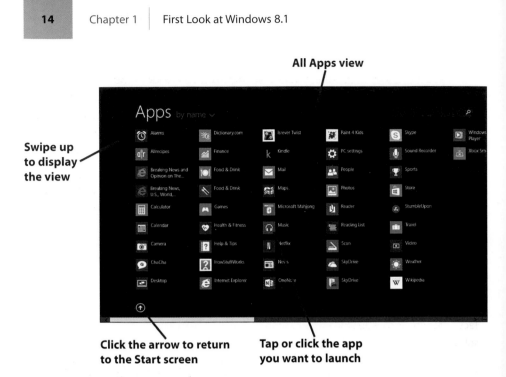

Click the arrow to return
to the Start screen

Tap or click the app
you want to launch

These items don't represent all there is to do in Windows 8.1, certainly, but they give you a quick bird's-eye view of some of the major places we'll be stopping along the way.

Using Touch in Windows 8.1

One of the biggest features Windows 8.1 offers is touch support. You've probably heard that you can tap, drag, flick, and pinch your new operating system to get it to do the things you most want it to do. That's a great change for Windows when you consider that we've been pointing and clicking mouse buttons for decades. One of the criticisms people offered about the initial release of Windows 8 is that it was *too* focused on touch. Folks who used the traditional desktop machine wondered what the operating system had to offer them. Now in Windows 8.1, Microsoft has tried to address that, but touch features are still a big focus of the operating system—and probably always will be.

Touch capability is no longer the wave of the future—it's the way many of us navigate our smartphones and tablets. In case you haven't noticed, human beings are touchy-feeling animals. We like to make good use of our fingers and opposable thumbs, and (or so my theory goes) we feel more in control of our world when we have a tactile sense that we are operating it correctly.

If you have a smartphone, you already know about touch. You tap the surface of your phone to dial a friend's number, you swipe through photos, you pinch a webpage to make the print larger (so you can read it on that small screen). Windows 8.1 even includes a "hands-free mode" for apps that support it.

The gestures you'll use on your tablet or multitouch monitor are similar to the ones you're probably already using on your smartphone. However, for good measure (and for those readers who don't go for the smartphones), let's go through the gestures you're likely to use most often in Windows 8.1.

Using Single Tap

You tap the screen to launch an app on the Windows 8.1 Start screen, select a setting, or choose an item to display.

1. Display the Windows Start screen or the app with the option you want to select.

2. Tap the display once quickly in the center of the tile or icon. If you tapped an application on the Start screen, the program opens; if you tapped a setting or an option, the item is selected or displays additional choices, if applicable.

Tap and Hold
If you want to select an item (and not activate it, as you did with the single tap) or perhaps display more information about an item, you can touch the item and hold your finger there until you see a small square surround the area. When you release your touch, a pop-up list of options appears. You can then tap the item you want to select.

Swiping Left

The swipe left gesture enables you to scroll screen quickly, from right to left and back again, and, if you're using Internet Explorer to browse the web, up and down as well.

1. Display the Windows 8.1 Start screen.

2. Touch a point toward the right side of the Start screen and drag to the left. The screen scrolls to the left, displaying additional apps.

Scroll Too Far?

One of the great things about touch is how natural it feels to make corrections. If you scroll the screen too far one way or another, simply reverse your swipe direction slightly to correct the display. It happens so easily you won't even have to think about it! Sweet.

Swiping Right

You use the swipe right gesture to cycle through open apps in Windows 8.1.

1. Display the Windows Start screen.

2. Launch at least two apps by tapping their tiles on the Start screen.

3. Drag in from left to right. The thumbnails pane appears on the left side of the Windows screen.

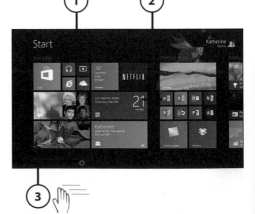

4. Drag the application you want to display from the thumbnails pane, and release it to replace the first open app with the second. You can repeat this gesture as needed and even keep more than one app open on the screen by positioning it where you want it to appear.

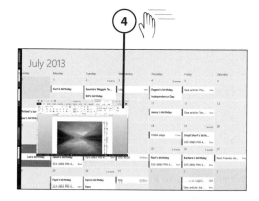

Working with Multiple Apps

You learn how to use Snap to place the apps on the screen in Chapter 5.

Docking Open Apps

You can continue scrolling through apps as long as you like; and you can also dock an app so that it stays visible in the Windows Start screen. You'll learn how to dock apps in Chapter 7.

Swiping Charm

When you swipe in from the right edge of your screen, the Charms bar appears, giving you the tools you need for searching for apps and files, sharing apps, choosing program settings, and using other devices.

Swiping Up and Down

The Windows 8.1 Lock screen gives you important information, even without unlocking your computer. You can see the small notification icons that tell you how much power your computer has, how strong your Internet connection is, how many emails you've received, and what you're appointments are for the afternoon. You can also add notifications for instant messages, calls, and more.

Swiping or clicking the Windows 8.1 Lock screen enables you to unlock your computer, select or close apps, and choose options.

1. To open the Windows 8.1 Lock screen, touch or click toward the bottom of the display. You can also press any key on your keyboard.

2. Drag up and the Lock screen image scrolls up off the screen, displaying your login screen.

3. When you're using an app, you can swipe down from the top of an app screen or up from the bottom to display options related to that app.

Options, Schmoptions

Don't be dismayed if the options you see available for the particular app you have open differ from those shown here. Different apps offer different choices. For example, the Calendar app gives you different choices than the Maps app does.

Options for
Weather app

Swipe Down to Close

One of the big criticisms of the early release of Windows 8 was that initially Windows developers didn't provide a way to close apps because Windows 8 actually suspends apps not in use. In Windows 8.1, you swipe down, from the top to the bottom of the screen, to close an open app.

Using Pinch Zoom

The Pinch Zoom gesture enables you to enlarge and reduce the size of the content on the screen. On the Start screen, for example, when you pinch your fingers together, you reduce the size of the tiles so that you can easily move them around or group them the way you want them. When you want to enlarge an area of the screen, you use your fingers to expand the area, and the screen magnifies along with your gesture.

1. Display the Start screen or the app you want to use.

2. Reduce the size of the content displayed by placing your thumb and forefinger on the screen and "pinching" the area together.

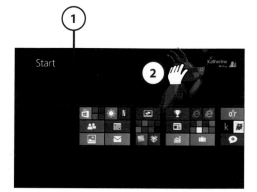

3. Enlarge an area of the screen by placing your thumb and forefinger together on the screen and expanding the distance between them.

Semantic Zoom

You might see this feature referred to as *semantic zoom*, so named because it enables you to magnify a specific region of the display without disturbing other parts of the screen. If the app you're using was designed for Windows 8.1, chances are that it supports the pinch zoom gesture. That means you can use two fingers to change the size of the content displayed on the screen.

>>>Go Further

INTRODUCING MICROSOFT SURFACE

On June 18, 2012, Microsoft unveiled the new Microsoft Surface, a state-of-the-art tablet with a built-in keyboard in the smartcover. Although you can use many tablets and touch devices with Windows 8.1, Microsoft Surface is optimized to work with the new operating system. Multiple touchpoints on the screen make navigating by touch as responsive and accurate as possible; and a live screen all the way out to the screen margins gives you the largest touch surface possible.

There are two versions of the Microsoft Surface. Surface RT runs on the ARM family of processors, which means that tablets based on the Android operating system can run Windows 8.1 and Word, Excel, PowerPoint, and OneNote in the RT versions successfully. The Windows 8.1 version of the Surface is based on the full version of the Microsoft operating system.

Getting Around with the Mouse and Keyboard

Windows 8 developers initially took a lot of heat when people realized that many of the best features in the new operating system seemed to be about the touch interface. People talked and wrote about the "split personality" of the operating system, and mouse users worried that opening and closing programs, working with files, and changing system settings would be more difficult if they opted not to use touch techniques to carry out the tasks.

As Windows has continued to evolve, however, Microsoft has made it clear that mouse users aren't being left in the dust. Windows 8.1 works equally well with touch, mouse, and keyboard.

Using the Mouse

The mouse can get you anywhere you want to go in Windows 8. Anything you can do with touch, you can do with your mouse—and then some. Whether you have a touch-capable device or not, you can still use your mouse for all the common tasks you'll perform in Windows 8.1: start apps, find and open files, and choose program settings. By now, this operation may be old hat, but here's a refresher.

Click a tile to launch an app

Scroll bar   **Display All Apps view**   **Click to move display screen**

- Move the mouse to the bottom of the Windows 8.1 Start screen. The horizontal scrollbar appears. You can click the right arrow to move the display one screen to the right.

- To see the options for an app in the lower-right corner of the Start screen, right-click an app tile. From there, you can click the option you want to use.

Right-click an app

App options appear

- Point to the upper-left corner of the screen to see a thumbnail of the most recently used app.

Most recently used app

- Click and drag the mouse down the left side of the screen to display the thumbnail strip of open apps. Click the app you want to display.

Thumbnails of open apps

Hands-Free Mode

Windows 8.1 includes a new hands-free mode that goes along with the Food and Drink app. This fascinating (and fun!) new "gesture" uses the webcam to enable you to swipe through pages without actually touching your tablet or touch device. This comes in handy when you are cooking and have dough all over your hands and don't want to get flour (or worse!) on your touchscreen.

First, you need to find and open the Food and Drink app if it isn't already on your Windows 8.1 Start screen. (Learn how to find and work with apps in Chapter 7.) Then start the app by tapping it on the Start screen.

Open a recipe you want to view, and tap Hands-Free Mode at the bottom of the screen. Windows 8.1 will ask whether you want to allow Bing Food & Drink to use your webcam and microphone: tap or click Allow.

A small Hands-Free ON symbol appears in the upper-right corner of the screen. Navigate by swiping your hand from right to left in front of your webcam; the gesture advances the pages in the direction you specify. The text in Hands-Free Mode is magnified so you can read it easily even if you're standing several feet away from your computer.

To turn off Hands-Free Mode, click the green Hands-Free indicator in the upper-right corner of the screen. Windows 8.1 disables the feature.

Hands-free mode

Hands-free mode uses the webcam to "see" your gestures.

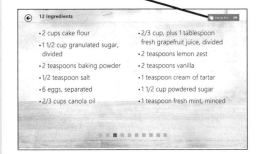

Selecting Multiple Items

In File Explorer, you can use the mouse and keyboard together to select multiple items at once. If you want to choose several files in a folder, for example, you can click the first item and then press and hold the Shift key and click the last item you want to select. All items between the two clicked items are selected.

If you want to select multiple items that aren't next to each other, click the first item and press and hold the Ctrl key; then click all the other items you want to include.

Mouse Shortcuts for Navigating Windows 8	
To do this:	**Do this:**
Unlock your Lock screen	Click any mouse button.
Display the Charms bar	Point to the upper- or lower-right corner of the Start screen.
Scroll the Start screen	Click and drag in the horizontal scrollbar at the bottom of the Start screen.
Show "power user menu"	Right-click the Windows 8.1 Start button in the lower-left corner of the Desktop or in the bottom of the thumbnails panel on the Start screen.
Display app options on the Start screen	Right-click the app tile.
Display app options in an open app	Right-click anywhere in the app window.
Show a thumbnail of the next app	Move the mouse to the upper-left corner to see the app that will appear when you drag in from the left edge of the screen.
Display a thumbnail strip of open apps	Point to the upper-left corner of the screen, and when the first thumbnail appears, drag the mouse down the left side of the screen; the thumbnail strip appears.

GETTING TO THE MENU

>>>Go Further

If you know what you're looking for in Windows 8 and want to get right to it, you might enjoy using what some people are calling the "power user menu" that appears when you right-click the new Start button in Windows 8.1. You can also display it by pressing Windows + X on your computer keyboard or your tablet's onscreen keyboard. The list of features includes many of those you might have been accustomed to working with in the Windows 7 Control Panel: Programs and Features, Mobility Center, Power Options, Device Manager, Run, and more. Click the feature you want to use, or, to hide the feature list, simply tap or click anywhere outside the list.

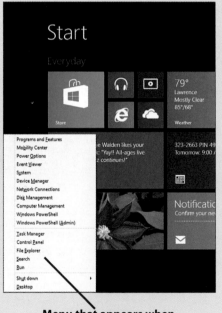

Menu that appears when you right-click the Start button in Windows 8.1

Using the (Real) Keyboard

For some of the things you'll do in Windows 8.1, you'll want a real, live keyboard. Sure you can type a quick memo or answer an email message on your tablet using the onscreen keyboard. But when you need to write a 10-page report for a departmental meeting or you have lots of work to do storyboarding the next team presentation, chances are you'll want to use a traditional keyboard with real keys to press.

In addition to using touch and the mouse, you can use your keyboard for navigating in Windows 8.1. When you use your keyboard to navigate the Start screen, move among apps, and manage windows, you use special keys, shortcut key combinations, and function keys.

Tab key   **Pg Up, Pg Dn keys**

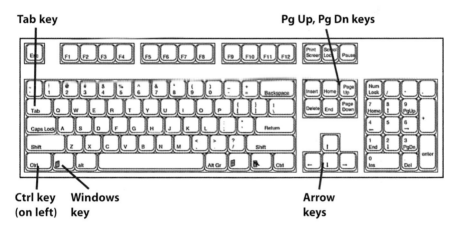

Ctrl key   Windows   Arrow
(on left)   key   keys

- The Windows key, commonly located on the lowest row of your keyboard on the left side between the Ctrl and Alt keys, takes you back to the Start screen no matter where you are in Windows 8.

- You can use the Pg Up and Pg Dn keys as well as the arrow keys to move among apps on the Windows 8 Start screen.

- You use the Tab key to move from option to option in a dialog box.

- You can press key combinations (such as Ctrl and the letter assigned to a specific menu option) to perform operations.

Keyboard Shortcuts for Navigating Windows 8.1	
To do this:	**Do this:**
Unlock your Lock screen	Press any key on the keyboard.
Display the Charms bar	Press and hold the Windows key and press C.
Display the Settings charm	Press Windows + I.
Show the Search charm	Press Windows + Q.
Switch between the Start screen and the Desktop	Press the Windows key.
Display the desktop	Press Windows + D.
Lock Windows 8.1	Press Windows + L.
Display power user commands	Press Windows + X.
Cycle through open apps	Press Windows + Tab.
Move to the next open app	Press Alt + Tab.

A Keyboard Is a Keyboard Is a Keyboard…Right?

Depending on the type of computer you are using, you might notice some differences in the ways certain keys appear on your keyboard. The keyboard mentioned here is a "basic" keyboard layout. Your keyboard might or might not have a separate numeric keypad, function keys across the top, and a set of cursor-control keys that are separate from the alphanumeric keys. Additionally, you may notice that your Delete key or Backspace key is in a slightly different place from other keyboards you see. Take the time to learn where to find the common keys on your Windows 8.1 keyboard—when you know the lay of the land, finding the right key at the right time will be second nature.

Using a Touch Keyboard

If you're using a touch device, you might not plan to type whole books on your onscreen keyboard, but it's nice to know you can use it in any way you need it. Windows 8.1 improves your typing experience by adding auto-text that offers word suggestions as you type; it also extends the function of the keyboard by including child keys that appear on the keyboard when you press and hold a specific key. This gives you easy access to the keys you need.

Begin by launching an app that will require you to type something on your tablet. For example, you might open the Mail app and start a new message. Then follow these steps to display and work with the Windows 8.1 touch keyboard:

1. Tap in the Subject area. The full keyboard appears along the bottom half of your screen.

2. Type the subject for the new appointment message. A gallery of words appears below the area where you type.

3. Swipe your finger on the onscreen spacebar to move the highlight and choose the word you want to use.

4. Press and hold a key to display child keys for some keys—for example, vowels that can have different accents, such as the vowels *a, e, i, o,* and *u* and punctuation characters like the period (.), apostrophe ('), and question mark (?).

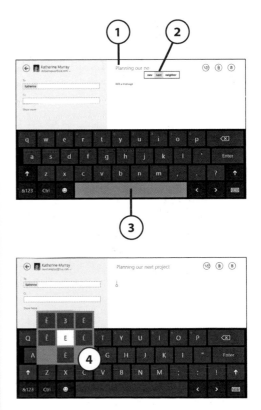

Choosing a Keyboard

Windows 8.1 offers several types of onscreen keyboards, and you can easily change the keyboard as you're using it. The standard keyboard offers all the basic keys you need and gives you the option of switching to show numbers and punctuation; the thumbs keyboard groups the keyboard on both sides of the screen so you can type with your thumbs on a tablet or other touch device. The extended keyboard displays all alphanumeric keys, as well as punctuation keys, Alt, Ctrl, and more.

Child Keys Aren't Available on the Extended Keyboard

If you want to use child keys on your onscreen keyboard, choose the standard or thumbs keyboard because they don't appear when you're using the extended keyboard.

1. If you want to change the type of keyboard displayed, tap the keyboard button in the lower-right corner of the keyboard.

2. A set of five choices appears. You can choose from the onscreen touch keyboard, a thumbs keyboard, a drawing tablet, the standard keyboard, or no keyboard. Tap the keyboard style you want to use.

3. The keyboard appears in the style you selected. Now you can type or draw your message.

Displaying the Standard Keyboard

The first keyboard option available to you displays the onscreen tablet keyboard, which doesn't include function keys or special keys such as the Windows key or Alt. The standard keyboard options are available to the left of the drawing pad icon, but if this keyboard isn't enabled in your PC settings, the item might be unavailable to you.

If the standard keyboard icon is grayed out, you can have Windows 8.1 display it as an option by swiping to display the Charms bar, tapping Settings, tapping Change PC Settings, selecting PC & Devices, and choosing Typing. Scroll down to the Touch Keyboard settings, and move the slider for the Add the Standard Keyboard Layout as a Touch Keyboard Option to the On position. When you return to the onscreen keyboard display, you'll now be able to select and use the standard keyboard as one of the key board options.

Resizing the Thumbs Keyboard

Windows 8.1 lets you change the size of the thumbs keyboard so that typing is as easy as possible. To display your sizing choices, tap the three vertical dots just to the right of the keyboard segment on the left side of the screen. Large is selected by default, but you can tap Small or Medium to change the size of the keyboard.

SAY WHAT?!

Windows 8.1 includes the Narrator accessibility feature, which reads the screen so people with visual challenges can interact successfully with Windows 8.1. Narrator offers natural-sounding voices (you can choose from three PC voices—two female voices and one male voice). You can also control the speed at which Windows 8.1 narrates your experience, which can be helpful if you're just learning how to use voice to navigate the operating system.

You can turn on Narrator as soon as you open the Lock screen, before you even log in to your computer. Simply tap the button in the lower-left corner of the login screen to begin the narration. You can also turn on Narrator by pressing and holding the Windows key and tapping the Volume Up button on your keyboard.

Internet Explorer 11 includes Narrator support as well, so users can listen to web content, understand links, and make choices about commands on webpages.

Finding the Help You Need

Developers of Windows 8.1 recognized another way they could help people be more successful with the new release: provide more obvious help support. Now instead of searching for help, Windows 8.1 Includes a Help & Tips app on the Start screen.

You can also still access Windows 8.1 Help and Support to find articles, tips, and troubleshooting techniques easily. If you've been looking for the little Help icon in Windows 8.1, you won't find it on the Start screen (it does still appear in File Explorer, though). But as you'll see, getting Help in Windows 8.1 is as easy as typing four little characters.

Using Windows 8.1 Help + Tips

In response to feedback from new users, Microsoft has included the Help + Tips app on the Windows 8.1 Start screen. When you launch the app by tapping or clicking it, the app offers you simple tutorials (complete with simple animations) on six different aspects of Windows 8.1: Start and Apps, Get Around, Basic Actions, Your Account and Files, Settings, and What's New.

Get Help + Tips

You'll find the Help + Tips app tile toward the right side of the Start screen. Launch the app by tapping or clicking the tile.

1. Tap or click Help + Tips.

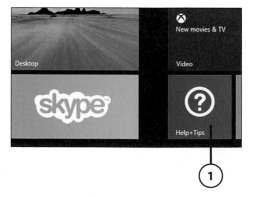

2. Tap the category that reflects the type of help you need.

3. Play a video to watch the demonstration of a technique.

4. Choose whether you want to navigate Help + Tips using touch or mouse.

5. Scroll to the right to display additional information.

6. Search for specific information on Windows.com.

7. When you're finished, swipe down to close the app.

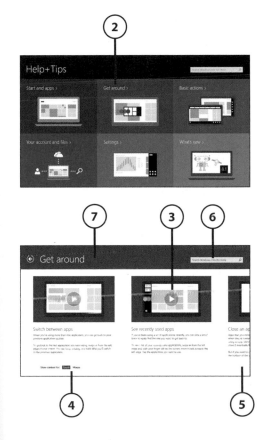

Displaying Windows Help and Support

What's the first thing to do when you feel like yelling "Help!"? How about this:

1. On your computer keyboard, type **hel**. Before you even get to the letter *p*, Windows 8.1 instantly opens a search and displays the characters you typed in the search box.

2. Tap or click Help and Support. The Windows Help and Support window appears.

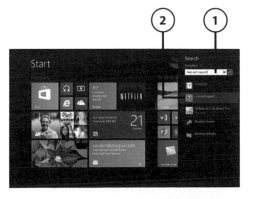

3. You can click one of the three displayed categories: Get Started; Internet & Networking; or Security, Privacy, & Accounts.

4. Or you can click in the Search box and type a word or phrase that reflects the type of information you want to find.

5. Click the Search tool.

6. Click a link to display a help article that looks as though it would offer the information you seek.

Changing Text Size

You can easily increase the text size in Help and Support by displaying the Windows Help and Support dialog box and then clicking Change Zoom Level in the lower-right corner of the Help window. Click Zoom In to magnify the text or Zoom Out to reduce the size of the text. You can also choose one of the other zoom percentages listed or click Custom to enter a zoom percentage of your own choosing.

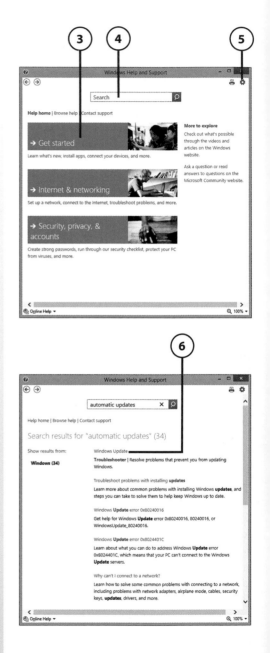

Printing Help

If you find that you are looking up a certain task repeatedly, you might want to print the help information to keep close to your computer until you commit it to memory.

1. Search for the help information you need.

2. Click Print at the top of the help window.

3. Choose your printer.

4. Set your print options.

5. Click Print.

Including Online Resources

To the right of the Print tool in the Help window, you'll find a Settings tool. When you click or tap that tool, the Help Settings dialog box appears, displaying two help settings: Get Online Help and Join the Help Experience Improvement Program, both of which are selected by default. The first option gives you access to the latest online help content when you search for help in Windows 8.1, and the second gives Microsoft permission to collect data about the way you're using the Help feature. If you don't want to send that type of information to Microsoft (even though you cannot be personally identified from the data collected), simply click to uncheck the box. Click OK to save any changes you made.

>>>Go Further

AND THAT'S JUST THE BEGINNING...

In addition to the help that's available to you in Windows 8.1 on your computer, you can visit Microsoft's Windows site (www.windows.microsoft.com) to learn more about Windows 8.1 features, watch videos, and learn about basic tasks.

Check out the Windows Community forums to find out what other users are asking about Windows 8. You'll see responses from Microsoft MVPs (Most Valuable Professionals) that might just help solve a problem you're having. Check it out if you have one of those hard-to-answer Windows 8.1 questions that has been keeping you awake at night.

Shutting Down or Putting Windows 8.1 to Sleep

Another common task you'll need to do regularly with Windows 8.1 is turn off your computer. Windows 8.1 does have a Shut Down tool, but it's not in an obvious place on the screen.

The secret is that Windows 8.1 tucks away the Shut Down command in the Settings charm in the Charms bar. You can easily turn off the computer—or just send it off to sleep—by selecting the option of your choice from the Settings charm.

Goodnight, Windows 8.1

When you're going to be away from your computer for a period of time but you aren't ready to turn everything off for the day, you can put your computer in Sleep mode to conserve energy and protect your files and programs while you're away.

1. Display the Charms bar by swiping left from the right edge of the screen or by pointing the mouse at the lower-right corner of the Start screen.

2. Tap or click Settings.

3. Tap or click Power. A list of options appears: Sleep, Shut Down, Restart.

4. Tap or click Sleep.

Wake Up, Little Fella

One of the great things about Sleep mode is that it is designed to help your computer spring back to life quickly as soon as you're ready. So even though it's a little distressing to see everything fade to black so quickly after you tap Sleep, you'll be pleased to know a simple tap of the Power button on your PC brings everything back to full wakefulness almost instantly.

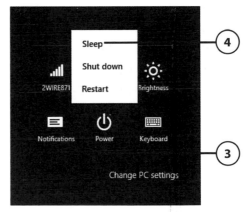

Shutting Down Windows 8

When you're ready to power down your computer, just tap or click Shut Down instead.

1. In the Settings charm, tap Power.

2. Tap or click Shut Down. If you have any open, unsaved files, Windows 8.1 prompts you to save them before shutting down.

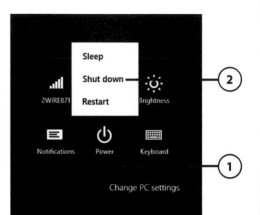

Starting Over

Of course, you have one more option when you tap or click the Settings charm and select Power. If you want to restart your computer, you can tap Restart; Windows 8.1 will power down and then reboot. You might be asked to restart your computer after you install an app or make a system setting change.

Windows 8.1 discovers and installs your devices automatically

Windows 8.1 finds the Internet connection options for you, and you can be online in seconds

This chapter helps you get your computer ready to use with the following tasks:

→ Adding devices in Windows 8.1
→ Connecting to wireless networks
→ Managing your PC power
→ Transferring files
→ Recovering your Windows 8.1

Preparing Your PC and Setting Up Devices

We live in an age of connected everything. We connect our phones and MP3 players and cameras to our PCs and tablets; we connect through the Web with computers we never see; we can access the file we left at home through the Web thanks to SkyDrive. The potential for connecting is almost limitless.

Windows 8.1 lets you easily prepare your PC and get things up and running. In Windows 8.1, Microsoft has rebranded Play To as Play and has changed the way you access this functionality from the Devices charm and pane. Fortunately, it's still pretty obvious.

First, you must ensure that the device you want to use for playback is connected to your PC. This happens in PC Settings, as before, but with the changes in 8.1, you'll need to do some extra digging, so navigate to PC & Devices and then Devices. Check your list of Play devices. If the device is present, you're good to go. Play, like Play To before it, remains mostly "dumb" in that it requires your PC to stay awake and on for the playback to work. That's because the content is streaming from the PC, not handing off playback as with Play On

Xbox. Put simply: A few UI changes have occurred, but everything basically works as before.

When you plug in a printer to your Windows 8.1 PC, the operating system automatically detects the printer and installs the necessary drivers. You can also set up devices that Windows 8.1 doesn't recognize right off the bat.

In addition to setting up your devices to work with Windows 8.1, you can add new wireless connections and choose a power management setting that helps you conserve energy without compromising performance power.

One other important aspect to preparing your PC involves knowing what to do if your computer begins behaving badly and you need to remove system changes or return to the way you'd previously configured it. Read on to finish preparing your Windows 8.1 PC so you can get on with all the fun stuff you want to do.

Adding Devices in Windows 8.1

Windows 8.1 includes an auto-discovery feature that scans for all devices connected to your PC or your network, detecting and connecting to printers, TVs, Xbox systems, and more. This means Windows 8.1 might be able to find and install all your computer peripherals automatically, without you needing to do anything at all! Wouldn't that be nice?

The first step involves using the Settings charm in the Charms bar to see which devices Windows 8.1 has already discovered and added to your system. You can then add a device if you have one that isn't included on the generated list.

Flummoxed by the Start Screen?

If you find the Windows 8.1 Start screen a bit overwhelming and you'd like to know more about the lay of the land before you begin changing settings, take a look at Chapter 3, "Using and Tweaking the Start Screen." That chapter introduces you to this important first screen and provides some basic navigational techniques (and some tweaks you can try) as you're acclimating to the new interface.

Viewing Installed Devices

You can take a look at the devices Windows 8.1 has found and installed automatically as part of your setup. And then, if needed, you can add a device or remove devices that were added but no longer need. To display the list, follow these steps:

1. On the Windows 8.1 Start screen, swipe in from the right or press Windows + C to display the Charms bar.

2. Tap or click Settings.

3. Tap or click Change PC Settings. The PC Settings window appears.

4. Tap or click PC and Devices in the categories on the left, and then choose Devices.

5. Review the devices that appear on the right side of the window.

Checking Device Status

Notice that for some of the devices in the list, a status indicator shows whether the device is ready, offline, or needs your attention. This helps you know, for example, whether your printer is turned on and ready to receive files you send to be printed.

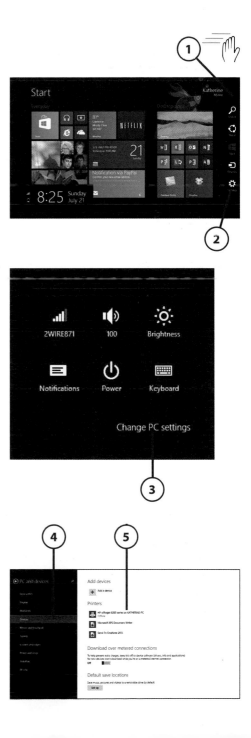

Adding a Device

If Windows 8.1 missed one of the devices you feel should be on the device list, you can scan again to see whether the device is discoverable. Before you tap or click Add a Device, be sure the device is connected to your computer or your home network and turned on. After you select Add a Device, Windows 8.1 scans your computer and shows any found devices in a pop-up list. You can then select the item you want to add to the Devices list in Windows 8.1.

Connecting a Device

You can also add a device by simply connecting it to your Windows 8.1 computer and letting Windows do the setup for you. For example, you might want to connect your MP3 player so that you can easily sync your podcasts and music.

1. With the Devices category selected in the PC and Devices screen, connect your device.

2. After a moment, Windows 8.1 displays the device in the Other Devices list.

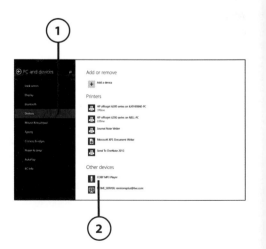

Connecting Unrecognized Devices

If you connect your device to Windows 8.1 and the operating system doesn't recognize the device you added, Windows 8.1 will display a message that setup needs to be finished in the Action Center. Click the link displayed in the message to go to the Action Center, and follow the steps to download and install it.

Removing a Device

You can remove a device you no longer need from the Devices list. Having extra devices in the Devices list doesn't do any harm, but if you want to keep the list short so you can easily find what you need, you might want to take any unnecessary items off the list.

1. Tap or click the device you want to remove from the list.

2. If you're sure you want to remove the device, tap or click the Remove Device button. Windows 8.1 removes the item from the list.

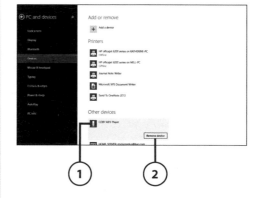

Troubleshooting Hardware Devices

Luckily, most of the time, your printer, router, scanner, camera, and drawing tablet function the way they're supposed to. You plug them in to your Windows 8.1 PC, Windows finds the right drivers, and they're ready for you to use. Simple.

But once in a while, devices have trouble. Your printer doesn't print anything. Your router is blinking, but you have no Internet connection. Windows 8.1 doesn't seem to be recognizing your MP3 player.

If you have trouble installing a device, you can use a Windows 8.1 troubleshooter to sleuth out the problem. Here are the steps:

1. On the Windows 8 Start screen, type **troubleshooter**. The Search pane appears.

2. Click Everywhere. A list of options appears.

3. Tap or click Settings.

4. Tap or click Find and Fix Problems. The Control Panel opens, displaying the Troubleshoot Computer Problems dialog box.

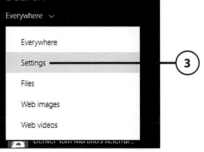

5. Tap or click Configure a Device. In the Hardware and Devices screen that appears, click Next to begin the troubleshooter. Windows 8.1 detects and then displays a report of findings. The type of information you see depends on the device you're using and the problems Windows 8.1 finds. When Windows 8.1 locates a problem, it asks whether you want to apply the selected fix or skip it.

6. Click or tap Apply This Fix to have Windows 8.1 take the suggested action.

7. Click or tap Skip This Fix if you want to bypass the suggestion and see another alternative. When the troubleshooter completes, a list of problems and actions is displayed.

8. If the troubleshooter didn't correct the problem you're having, tap or click the View Solution button and review the information displayed on the Message Details screen.

9. Click Additional Info to get further information about the issue Windows 8.1 has found.

10. Click or tap the Close box to close the troubleshooter.

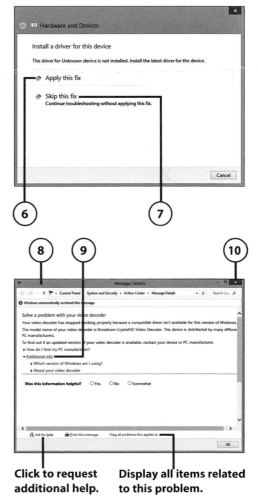

Click to request additional help.

Display all items related to this problem.

>>> Go Further

STILL YELLING HELP

If you've been through the troubleshooter and tried exploring additional options and nothing is fixing the problem you're having, you can search online for help in the Windows Community, available at www.windows.microsoft.com. In addition to other Windows users, you'll find Microsoft Most Valuable Professionals (MVPs) who might be able to offer insight into the problem you're having. You also might be able to find a fix to the problem by searching for information about it using your favorite search engines.

Additionally, you can visit the website of the hardware manufacturer to see whether there are any known fixes for your particular issue. You might find it's something as simple as a driver that needs updating, and the manufacturer site will be able to walk you through that process (or help you connect with tech support in some way).

Connecting to Wireless Networks

Today, we're almost *always* connected. We go from the corporate network at work to Bluetooth or mobile connectivity on the road to Wi-Fi at the neighborhood coffee shop. Windows 8.1 makes the change right along with you, discovering networks in your area and giving you the ability to connect (if you have the password or network key, of course) by simply tapping the connection you want to make. You can easily switch among networks by using the Networks tool in the Settings charm.

Connecting to an Available Network

Your first step to getting online involves taking a look at all the networks Windows 8.1 is aware of and choosing the one you want to use.

1. Swipe left, or point the mouse to the lower-right corner of the Start screen to display the Windows 8.1 Charms bar.

2. Tap or click Settings.

3. Tap or click the network icon displaying your current Internet connection. Windows 8.1 lists all network connections in your area.

4. Tap or click the connection you want to change.

5. If you want Windows 8.1 to connect to the network automatically whenever it's present, click or tap the Connect Automatically check box.

6. Tap or click Connect to connect to the network immediately. Similarly, if you want to disconnect from a network to which you're connected, tap or click the Disconnect button.

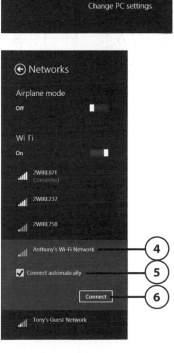

>>>Go Further

REPAIRING NETWORK CONNECTIONS

If for some reason you're having trouble connecting to the Internet, Windows 8.1 can help you identify the problem and correct it. On the Windows 8.1 Start screen, begin typing **repair network**.

The results list shows Identify and Repair Network Problems. Tap or click the tool to launch Windows Network Diagnostics and a troubleshooting tool that investigates the connection problem. Complete any steps as suggested by the troubleshooter; if no problems are found, the troubleshooter lets you know and offers the Close button so you can end the utility with no further action.

Managing Your PC Power

Thankfully, as computer makers continue to improve the hardware they offer, our computers and devices are becoming more energy efficient. This is good not only for our bank accounts, but also for our planet. We want the batteries in our laptops, tablets, and smartphones to last as long as possible. The more power we conserve, the longer our power lasts—and that's a good thing.

One thing we've learned in green tech is that small changes can make a big difference. Changing the brightness of your screen, or turning off Wi-Fi or roaming when you can, can save a lot of processing going on behind-the-scenes. Even reducing energy consumption on your home desktop PC can have tangible benefits, like reducing your electric bill. Those simple techniques, added to steps like thinking through what happens when you close your laptop cover, can add up to smarter energy use for us all.

Windows 8.1 is the most energy-efficient version of Windows yet, with careful attention paid to apps that are in the foreground. Apps that cycle to the background and go into suspended mode have no impact on power usage at all. And because Windows 8.1 boots so efficiently, you won't experience any lag time while you wait for an app you select to load. That's a big change from the days you could push the power button and then go to the kitchen to get a cup of coffee while waiting for your computer to boot up.

Choosing a Power Management Plan

Windows 8.1 supports the same power management plans that were available in Windows 7. The Balanced power plan balances usage with performance, and Power Saver reduces computer performance a bit to lower your energy use. Selecting a plan is as simple as pointing and clicking.

1. On the Start screen, type **power plan**.

2. Click Choose a Power Plan. The Power Options dialog box appears.

3. Click the power plan you want to use.

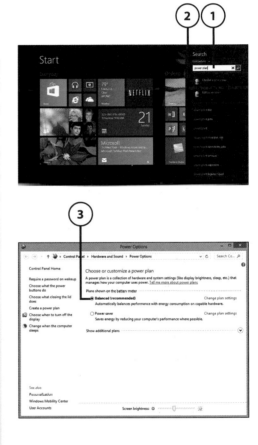

Wait, Reverse That

If you change the power settings and then have second thoughts and want to undo your changes, you can click the Restore Default Settings for This Plan link that appears in the same window where you modify the plan settings. Windows 8.1 returns the plan to its default settings.

Screen's So Bright I Gotta Wear Shades

One easy way to save some power right off the bat is to click the slider in the Screen Brightness control at the bottom of the Power Options dialog box and drag it to the left. This dims the display relative to the slide setting on the bar. This setting is applied to all of Windows, so your apps will reflect the same level of screen brightness you set here. You can change the brightness level at any time by returning to this screen and adjusting the brightness level more to your liking.

Changing Power Settings

Each of the power management plans you can choose with Windows 8.1 enables you to set priorities about the way you use Windows 8.1 and the type of power you use and save. For example, you can choose a plan that saves as much power as possible or select a plan that balances the power use with your computer's performance.

You can view and change the settings to fit the plan you have in mind and tweak individual settings along the way.

1. On the Start screen, type **power options**.

2. Tap or click Power Options.

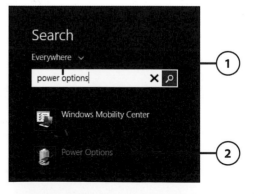

3. Click or tap the setting you want to change. Different dialog boxes will appear depending on the option you select. The System Settings dialog box appears when you choose either Change What the Power Buttons Do or Change What Closing the Lid Does.

4. Choose whether you want your computer to sleep, hibernate, shut down, or do nothing when you press the power button. Select the setting first for your computer when it is running on battery and then when it is plugged in.

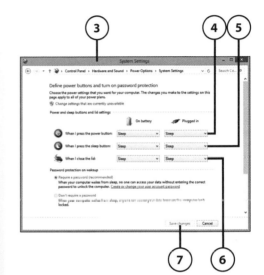

5. Select what you want the computer to do when you press the sleep button in battery and plugged-in modes.

6. Choose what you want the computer to do when you close the computer lid (again, for both battery and plugged-in scenarios).

7. Click Save Changes.

Transferring Files

If your new Windows 8.1 computer is the latest in a line of computers you've used at home or at work, it's likely that you have files you'd like to transfer from one computer to another. How do you move the things you most need to be able to carry on your work? You have a few options:

- Use Windows Easy Transfer.

- Save the files to Microsoft SkyDrive or another online storage space.

- Add both computers to your home network and transfer files from one to the other.

You'll learn about saving files to Microsoft SkyDrive, setting up a home network, and establishing a Homegroup in Chapter 12, "Working in the Clouds," so this section focuses on using Windows Easy Transfer to move files and folders from your old computer to your new one.

Transferring Programs

The process for moving programs from one computer to another sometimes involves uninstalling the program on one computer and installing it on the new one, due to the licensing issues involved in legal copies of software you might have purchased. Some programs enable you to log in to your account online and download the software from the company's website. Be sure to gather the following information from programs on your old PC before you uninstall the programs:

- Your user ID and password
- Your software registration number
- Any toll-free numbers or websites related to the software
- Any identifying information that shows your legitimate ownership of the software

Using Windows Easy Transfer

Windows Easy Transfer transfers files, settings, Internet favorites, email, and more from your old computer to your new one. Before you begin using the utility, log in to both computers as an administrator and make sure both have Windows Easy Transfer installed. (If not, you can download the tool from the Microsoft Downloads site.)

Begin by using Windows Easy Transfer on your old computer to prepare a transfer file that you can then install on your new Windows 8.1 PC. Then, when you have saved the transfer file (you can use these steps for both computers), add the transferred files to your computer by following these steps:

1. On your existing computer, search for **Windows Easy Transfer**.

2. Tap or click it in the results list.

3. Skip past the Welcome to Windows Easy Transfer screen by clicking Next; on the next screen, choose Yes to tell Windows 8.1 you have the files from your old computer ready to transfer. The Open an Easy Transfer File dialog box appears.

4. Choose the drive where your file is stored.

5. Select the folder containing the file.

6. Tap or click the file and click Open. Windows. This makes the connection and begins copying the files from one system to another (if you elected to transfer files over your network). When the transfer process is complete, your files will be installed and ready to use on your Windows 8.1 PC.

Checking Administrator Status

To make sure you're logged in as the administrator, type User Accounts on the Windows 8.1 Start screen; then tap or click User Accounts. Your user account appears, listing the account type assigned to your account. If you need to change the setting, click or tap Change Your Account Type and select Administrator. Then click or tap Change Account Type to save your change.

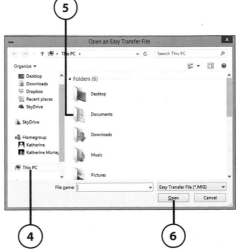

>>>Go Further

CHOOSING THE RIGHT TRANSFER METHOD

Windows Easy Transfer gives you three ways to transfer your files, depending on the type of setup you have and how you want to copy the files:

- If you bought an Easy Transfer cable when you purchased your computer, you can use it to connect the two systems you'll be using to transfer the files. (Note that this is not a standard Universal Serial Bus [USB] cable. You can purchase an Easy Transfer cable online or by visiting your local electronics store.)

- If you've set up a home network and both computers are part of the network, you can transfer files as easily as you would copy them from one folder to another. You learn more about home networks in Chapter 12.

- You can also use a USB flash drive or an external hard drive to store the file Windows Easy Transfer prepares for you. You can then move the flash drive or external hard drive to the new computer and transfer the files.

Recovering Your Windows 8.1

We all know—only too well—that computers sometimes have their off days. Things slow to a crawl. Your apps hang up. Programs aren't launching the way they should.

If you're having problems consistently, Windows 8.1 gives you a tool that can make things better quickly and easily. Now, instead of crossing your fingers and rebooting—or perhaps arbitrarily choosing a Restore Point and hoping your journey back in time will fix the trouble you're having—you can use Windows Refresh to simply refresh your Windows 8.1 installation without wiping away any files or settings. Or, if necessary, you can reinstall Windows 8.1 and return your computer to its pristine, out-of-the-box state.

Refreshing Your PC

If you find that a few of your apps aren't working the way they should or your computer has been behaving unreliably, you can refresh your computer to restore the program files and settings to their original state without losing your files, media, and settings.

1. On the Start screen, display the Charms bar.

2. Tap or click Settings.

3. Tap or click Change PC Settings. The PC Settings screen appears.

4. Select Update & Recovery from the list on the left.

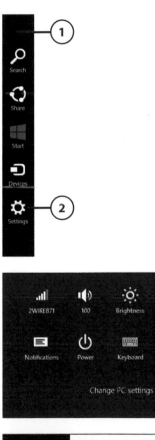

5. Tap Recovery. Windows 8.1 displays three options.

6. Click the top Get Started button if you want to refresh your PC without losing any of your files or data.

7. Click the second Get Started button to reset your PC to the factory settings (which means that your files and data will be wiped clean).

8. Click Restart Now to boot Windows from a USB drive or DVD or to restore your files from a system image you've previously saved.

USING THE WINDOWS MOBILITY CENTER

>>>Go Further

If you are looking for one central location where you can go to find the settings that control the way you use your computer on the road, you don't need to look any further than the Windows Mobility Center. You can display the center by typing Windows Mobility Center on the Start screen and tapping or clicking the app to open the Windows Mobility Center window.

You can change options for Brightness, Volume, Battery Status, Screen Orientation, External Display, Sync Center, and Presentation Settings in the Windows Mobility Center. Simply tap or click the control of the item you want to change and select your choice.

If you use the Windows Mobility Center often, add it to the Start screen so you can reach it easily by swiping the app or right-clicking it. Then choose Pin to Start to add it as a tile on your Start screen.

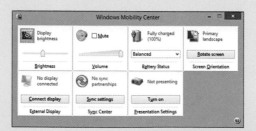

The Windows 8.1 Start
screen gives you access to
apps, tools, and more.

You can display Apps
view easily in Windows
8.1 by swiping up on the
Start screen or clicking
the down arrow.

In this chapter, you get going with Windows 8.1 by using and personalizing the Start screen. Along the way, you'll try these tasks:

→ Beginning with the Start screen
→ Checking out the charms
→ Changing the way tiles look and behave
→ Moving, grouping, and removing apps
→ Searching in Windows 8.1

Using and Tweaking the Start Screen

You've probably heard mixed reports about the Windows 8.1 Start screen—that colorful, moving surface that displays your favorite apps so you can reach them easily. Like many of the new features in Windows 8, public reaction has been mixed: some people love the new approach, and other people…well, not so much.

The idea behind the Start screen is that it is a beautiful, tappable, customizable surface on which you can display all the apps that matter most to you so that you can launch them easily and get right into the program or media you are hoping to enjoy. What's more, some of the apps you use have what's called *live tiles* that update information in real time so you can stay up-to-date (on how many emails you have received, for example) without actually opening the app. The operating system fades to the background by putting your apps front and center.

But for years, we've been using a version of Windows that requires a fair amount of management. We selected programs from menu lists. We were familiar with a two- or three-step process as we found the files we wanted to work with. This new tap-and-go approach is jarring for many.

So during the Windows 8.1 Preview, Microsoft announced the return of a Start button. Notice that I didn't say it's *the* Start button, as in the one we were accustomed to in Windows 7. The new Start button in Windows 8.1 provides an easy way to move from the desktop to the Start screen. If you right-click it, you will see a menu that contains options to get you into what Microsoft thinks of as "power user" tools: Programs and Features, Mobility Center, Device Manager, Task Manager, and more.

This chapter introduces you to the Windows 8.1 Start screen and shows you how you can tweak it to get just the mix of touch- or clickability and menuing you're looking for. If you just want to use the Start screen as is, no problem! You'll find what you need to know in the tasks covered in this chapter.

Looking for Start Screen Makeovers?

If you want to change the background of the Start screen, the Windows Desktop, and the Lock Screen, check out Chapter 5, "Making It *Your* Windows 8.1," where we cover all the great ways you can personalize Windows 8.1.

Beginning with the Start Screen

Microsoft likes practical names. The Lock screen is the first screen you see when you power up your computer or device—so named because, of course, your computer is locked until you enter your password or PIN. The Start screen is named the way it is because this is where all your work and play with Windows 8.1 really begins (although you can change that if you'd like, which we cover later in this chapter).

Chances are good, though, that your first exploration with Windows 8.1 will begin with the Start screen. You'll find lots of information in this colorful display, as well as access to Windows tools you need to tweak your settings and personalize your Windows 8.1 experience.

What's the Difference Between an App and a Program?

Yes, new lingo comes with the territory on Windows 8.1. Actually an app *is* a program, but now we're saying it in a hipper, cooler way. An app might also mean a smaller, more focused tool, like a photo app or a calendar app, that instead of doing everything under the sun focuses on doing one thing really well. That being said, however, you'll notice that bigger desktop programs that run on your Windows 8.1 Desktop—such as Microsoft Office—are still called *applications* or, sometimes, *apps*.

The Start screen gives you access to apps on your Windows 8.1 computer and lets you easily get to the programs you use most often. All the apps you have installed don't appear on the Start screen by default, however. (You can choose which apps you want to display.)

You'll discover when you first fire up your Windows 8.1 PC or tablet that a number of apps appear by default, but you can also add apps, create new groups or apps, and remove apps you don't think you'll need from the Start screen.

Also from app tiles on the Start screen, you can display the Windows desktop, get to your photos or music, begin browsing with Internet Explorer 11, or start shopping in the Windows Store.

What Time Is It, Anyway?

In previous versions of Windows, we've counted on the taskbar to show us the time of day and the date, but you'll notice in Windows 8.1 that time and date information is conspicuously missing from the Start screen display. You can find out what time it is (and get other information, too, such as how strong your Internet connection is or how much power your laptop has) by swiping in from the right edge of the screen or positioning the mouse in the upper-right corner. This displays the Windows 8.1 Charms bar; the system information icons, time, and date appear on the left side of the Start screen.

Viewing All Your Apps at Once

If you don't see on the Start screen a specific app you want to use—Windows Paint, for example—you can display Apps view to find the app and launch it easily. You wouldn't want to have every app on your Start screen, anyway, because you could be scrolling for a long time to find the app tile you need.

Now in Windows 8.1, Microsoft has made it easy to get a quick look at all the apps you have installed. And even better, you can launch the app from that same view. This view, called Apps view, is available whenever you swipe up on the Start screen or position the mouse in the lower-left corner so that the down-arrow appears.

1. Swipe up on the Windows 8.1 Start screen, or click the down-arrow tool. Apps view appears.

2. Swipe the screen, or use your mouse to browse through all the available apps.

3. If you want to launch an app, tap or click it.

4. Type an app name to use search to locate the app.

Fast and Easy App Finding

Another quick way to move from the Start screen right to the app you need is to just begin typing the app name on your keyboard. This ignites Windows 8.1's lightning-fast search, and you can launch the program by simply tapping or clicking the tile Windows 8.1 presents. You'll learn more about search later in this chapter.

Reordering Apps in Apps View

Apps view shows all the apps that are installed in Windows 8.1 on your computer or device. At first, Windows 8.1 lists the apps by name, in alphabetical order; but you can change that. You can click or tap the arrow to the right of By Name to display a list of additional options and choose the way you want the apps to appear.

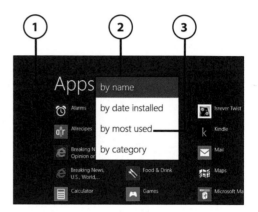

1. Display Apps view by swiping up on the Start screen or clicking the down-arrow tool.

2. Click or tap the down-arrow to the right of Apps By Name at the top of the screen.

3. Choose the option that reflects the way you want the apps to be displayed: By Name, By Date Installed, By Most Used, or By Category.

Tweaking the Start Screen

One of the ways Microsoft improved Windows 8.1 was to give users more choice over the way the Start screen looks and operates. On some displays, you can increase the number of app tiles displayed on the screen (which means you don't have to scroll to the right forever) and further customize the display by selecting from a variety of app tile sizes.

It's Good to Have Options

Not every computer screen or tablet is capable of taking advantage of the new tile features in Windows 8.1. The operating system prefers high-resolution screens (for example, 1280×800). So how will you know whether you can use these new features? Don't worry—Windows 8.1 knows for you. If you can't use the new features, they will be grayed out on your machine and you won't be able to select them. Which is a bummer, I know.

Showing More Tiles

Now in Windows 8.1, you can display more tiles on the Start screen and make the most of the screen real estate. By default, Windows 8.1 shows tiles three rows deep, but selecting Show More Tiles adds a fourth row.

1. On the Start screen, display the Charms bar.

2. Click or tap the Settings charm.

3. Click or tap Tiles. The Tiles settings appear.

4. Slide the Show More Tiles slider to Yes. The app tiles on the Start screen are resized and rearranged.

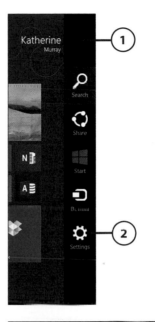

OH, THE GLORY OF THE ADMINISTRATOR

>>>Go Further

In the Tiles pane of the Settings charm, you can also display administrative tiles, if you are the lucky person responsible for watching over the health of the system (for yourself or your department). That's just a simple flip of the Show Administrative Tools switch in Windows 8.1, as you can see.

So what kind of special privileges are you in for, now that you've displayed the Administrative tools? If you swipe up or click the arrow to display All Apps view, you'll see that the operating system has added several tools for you: Event Viewer, Task Scheduler, Resource Monitor, Local Security Policy, Performance Monitor, Component Services, Computer Management, Disk Cleanup, Defragment and Optimize Drives, iSCSI Initiator, System Configuration, ODBC Data Sources, Windows Memory Diagnostic, System Information, Print Management, Services, Windows PowerShell ISE, and Windows Firewall with Advanced Security.

I know, I know! You'd better skip lunch today. You have way more important stuff to do. Or, if you're rather not deal with all this serious business right now while you're learning (and a bit enchanted by) all the color and movement in Windows 8.1, you can hide the Admin tools and come back to them in Chapter 13, "Care, Feeding, and Troubleshooting." For most day-to-day operations, you don't really need access to these tools, anyway, so you might want to hide them to keep them from cluttering up your Start screen.

Diving Deeper into Windows 8.1

This chapter shows you how to use the Start screen as the starting point for the apps you'll use in Windows 8.1, but later chapters in the book go into more detail on the specific tools. For example, you'll learn more about working with the Windows 8.1 desktop in Chapter 4, "Working with the Desktop"; browsing for new apps in Chapter 7, "Diving in with Apps"; working with the File Explorer to manage files and folders in Chapter 8, "Organizing Files with File Explorer"; and beginning to browse in Chapter 9, "Browsing with Internet Explorer 11."

Checking Out the Charms

Keeping the Start screen sleek and simple is one objective, but how do we get to the tools we need when we need them? The Windows 8.1 Charms bar is Microsoft's answer to that question. Charms provide easy access to the tools we need without cluttering up the Start screen.

If you're using a touch-capable monitor or device, you can display the Charms bar by swiping from the right edge of the screen toward the center. If you're using a mouse, you can display the Charms bar by pointing to the upper- or lower-right corner of the Start screen. The charms give you access to various tools that enable you to tweak different aspects of Windows 8.1.

A Ghost of a Charms Bar

If you're using the mouse, when you position the pointer in the upper- or lower-right corner of the screen, you see the white outlines of the charms, but the whole Charms bar doesn't appear until you move the mouse into the Charms bar area. Then the black background appears and you see the full effect of the Charms bar.

Displaying the Charms Bar

The Charms bar appears on both the Start screen and the Desktop in Windows 8.1. You can display the Charms bar by using touch or the mouse, and you can easily get to the charms whenever you need them.

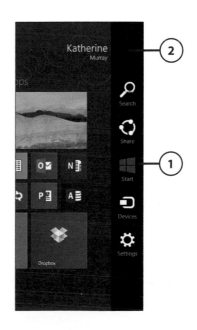

1. Using touch, swipe in from the right side of the Start screen or Desktop.

2. Or, click in the upper- or lower-right corner of the Start screen or desktop.

A Shortcut, If You Please

If you'd rather not take your hands off the keyboard, you can display the Charms bar by pressing Windows + C.

Choosing Your Charm

After the Charms bar is displayed, you can tap or click the charms you want to change. The charms available to you are the following:

- **Search**—Enables you to search for all sorts of content (apps, files, settings, images, and more) on your computer or on the web. You can also search *within* apps.

- **Share**—Enables you to share photos, links, and more with other people. Begin by choosing the item you want to share, and then swipe in and tap Share to see a list of ways you can share the item you've selected.

- **Start**—Returns you to the Windows Start screen, which, of course, is helpful only if you aren't already on the Windows Start screen.

- **Devices**—Gives you the option of connecting to a device recognized by Windows 8.1.

- **Settings**—Enables you to personalize Windows 8.1, change the way your tiles look, or get help. You can also change the way your system is functioning, such as changing your network connection or adjusting the brightness and volume of your computer. You have access to a world of PC settings by selecting the Change PC Settings link at the bottom of the Settings pane. You can also display help information and change the information on your app tiles by using the Settings charm.

Search for apps, settings, files, images, videos, and more

Share files, photos, and links with others

Display the Windows 8.1 Start screen

Connect to other devices

Change Windows 8.1 settings

Where Are My Devices?

If you don't see a device in the Device charm you want to use, make sure you've installed it in Windows 8.1. To get the how-to for that task, see Chapter 2, "Preparing Your PC and Setting Up Devices."

SILLY RABBIT, CHARMS AREN'T FOR KIDS!

>>>Go Further

One of the neat things about the Charms bar is that it is context-dependent, meaning that the Settings you see when you tap the Settings charm depend on what you're viewing in the rest of your Windows 8.1 screen. If you tap Settings when you're looking at your Photos app, for example, you'll see the categories Settings, About, Help, Permissions, and Rate and Review. If you tap Settings when you're instant messaging a colleague, you'll see Account, Options, Permissions, and Rate and Review categories.

So even though the charms can appear to be consistent no matter where you display them or what you're doing at the time, know that Windows 8.1 is tailoring the options you're seeing—in Search, Share, Devices, and Settings—to fit the context of what you're working on.

Changing the Way Tiles Look and Behave

You might be wowed when you first begin working with the Start screen, but sooner or later you're going to start wondering how to change things. You might want to make some of the app tiles larger or smaller, or turn on—or off—those scrolling updates that let you know about new mail messages, Facebook updates, and more. Luckily, Windows 8.1 includes a number of tools you can use to tweak the way your tiles behave.

Making Big Tiles Small (and Vice Versa)

As you've no doubt noticed by now, app tiles on the Windows 8.1 Start screen vary: some are large and some are small. You can reduce the size of the large app tiles on the Start screen if you want to condense the number of apps that appear in the various groups. This lets you easily fit more apps on one screen area so you can see them without scrolling.

1. To change the size of a large tile, tap and hold the tile or right-click it to select it. The apps bar appears along the bottom of the screen and a checkmark appears in the upper-right corner of the tile, showing that it is selected.

2. If the large app allows you to change the tile size, you'll see a Resize option. If no Resize setting appears, it means that setting isn't available for that app.

3. Tap the size you want to select for that app tile. You might see Wide, Medium, or Small.

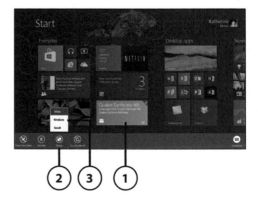

Turning Off Live Updates

You can also turn off the live tile updates for a particular tile if you like by selecting the tile (by tapping and holding it or right-clicking it) and then tapping or clicking Turn Live Tile Off in the apps bar at the bottom of the screen. To turn on the live updates later, simply reselect the app tile and tap Turn Live Tile On.

It's Not All Good

BORING APP TILES

You might get a trade-off for changing your app tiles from large to small. If the tile previously displayed app notifications (meaning the information on the tile updated automatically), the live notifications might disappear, depending on whether the app has been programmed to provide updates in both sizes.

Choosing New App Tile Sizes

Another change in Windows 8.1 is the welcome addition of new tile sizes—for some of us. Similar to the tile display on Windows Phone, now Windows 8.1 can display a variety of sizes beyond small and large. To make this change, you'll need to go into PC Settings; don't worry, though, that's just a few taps away:

1. On the Start screen, display the Charms bar.

2. Click or tap the Settings charm.

3. Click or tap Change PC Settings. The PC settings screen appears.

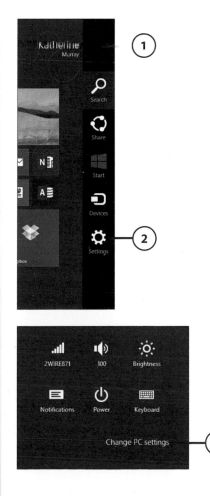

4. Tap or click PC and Devices.

5. Tap or click Display.

6. Tap or click the More Options arrow.

7. Choose the setting you prefer from the list that appears.

It's Not All Good

TILE SIZES FOR THE HAVE-NOTS

Yes, those of us who don't have the necessary screen resolution to tweak our app tile sizes as we like have been left out in the cold. And there's not much we can do to change that, beyond purchasing a monitor or device with better screen resolution. Changing the Resolution setting on the PC & Devices page won't do the trick, and changing from Landscape to Portrait will leave you disappointed.

We can hope that as Microsoft continues to add support for additional devices and screen sizes, they'll remember those of us with small tablets who'd like a little variety, too.

Getting a Rest from Notifications

Suppose that a deadline is hanging over your head; you've had too much coffee; and the rotating, flipping updates on the Windows Start screen are making you crabby. Notifications push new information to the live tiles on your Windows Start screen. You can choose to turn them off for a while so they'll stop distracting you. Here's how to do that:

1. On the Windows Start screen, swipe in from the right side of the screen or point to the upper- or bottom-right corner to display the Charms bar.

2. Tap Settings.

3. Tap Notifications. A pop-up list appears, giving you the option of hiding the live tile notifications for 8 hours, 3 hours, or 1 hour.

4. Tap or click the setting you'd like to apply. Now you won't see new information for the period of time you've selected.

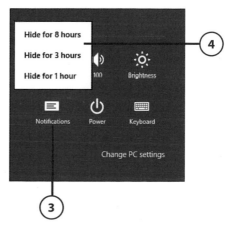

A Little Less Lively

After you reduce the size of a large app tile, you might notice something you're not too crazy about: apps that previously functioned as live tiles, providing continually updating information, now simply display a logo. The "aliveness" is gone. Windows 8.1 does allow developers to create live tiles for the smaller, square tile, but fitting updating information into that small space is a bit of a challenge. Therefore, at this point, most live tiles are of the larger variety. When you want to restore the tile to its larger, livelier state, simply swipe down on the tile or right-click it and click or tap Resize in the apps bar; then select the size you want the tile to be.

Hiding Personal Information on Your Tiles

If you regularly share your computer with someone else or have people forever looking over your shoulder (doesn't that bug you?), you can have Windows 8.1 hide the personal information on your tiles.

1. On the Windows Start screen, swipe in from the right or point the mouse to the upper- or lower-right corner to display the Charms bar.

2. Tap or click Settings.

3. Tap or click Tiles.

4. Tap Clear. Tiles such as Mail, Messaging, and Calendar, which had been showing your latest email messages, instant messages, and upcoming appointments, now should display the plain-Jane app logos instead. So, those folks looking over your shoulder won't be able to see much.

← Tiles

Show more tiles
No

Show administrative tools
No

Clear personal info from my tiles
Clear — **4**

For One Brief Shining Moment

It's important to realize, however, that your live tiles—if you haven't turned off the live tile at this point—will continue to display your personal information as you receive new email messages, instant messages, and appointments. If you want to suppress the display of personal information for a longer period, such as the entire time you're at work, turn off notifications for eight hours or turn off the live tile display.

Moving, Grouping, and Removing Apps

Another way you can tweak the Windows 8.1 Start screen and make it yours involves moving apps around on the screen, grouping them in ways that make sense to you, or removing the ones you don't need. (Don't worry, if you remove an app from the Windows 8 Start screen, you aren't actually removing it from your computer altogether; you are simply taking it off the Start screen.)

Installing and Uninstalling Apps

You will learn how to download, install, and uninstall apps when you take a closer look at them in Chapter 7.

Moving Apps on the Start Screen

You can rearrange the apps on your Start screen if you want to put them in a specific order that better suits the way you work. For example, one of my pet peeves is having wide and square tiles arranged on top of each other, resulting in blank space in the columns. So, I rearrange things to make the best use of space. The nice thing in Windows 8.1 is that you can put them in any order that suits you.

1. Select the app you want to move by pressing and holding the app.

2. Drag the app tile to the new location.

3. Release the app tile, and the other app tiles are rearranged to make room for the new app tile position.

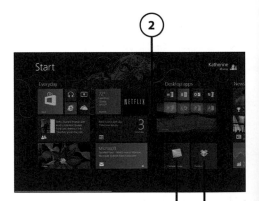

Creating an App Group

You'll notice that the Windows 8.1 Start screen includes a couple of "islands" of app tiles, and some are grouped together with a little space between groups. You can change the way the groups are organized by moving app tiles from one group to another. You can also create your own groups, which is a great idea if you have a set of apps you use often together. After you create a group, you can name it so that you can remember at a glance how you've grouped the apps on the Start screen.

1. Click or tap the tile you want to move.

2. Drag it to the space between one of the app groups on the Start screen, and release the tile. A horizontal bar appears to show you where the tile will be placed when you release it.

3. Grab other apps, drag them to the same space, and release them. Windows adds space around the group so that you can see it easily as a group.

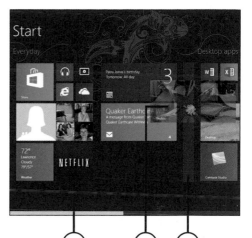

Making It All Fit

You can easily resize the app tiles after you add them to the new group by selecting the app tile and choosing Resize in the Apps bar. Then select the size you want the tile to be; Windows 8.1 rearranges the tiles in the group for you.

Naming App Groups

After you've created your app groups, you can further organize them by assigning a group name that appears on the Start screen. You can give your groups any name you like and change the name as often as it suits you.

1. On the Start screen, swipe up from the bottom of the screen, or right-click a blank area on the screen.

2. Tap or click Customize.

3. Tap or click the name area of the group you want to change. A text box opens and, if you're using a tablet, the onscreen keyboard appears.

4. Type a name for the group.

5. Tap or click outside the text box. The name appears above the group you selected.

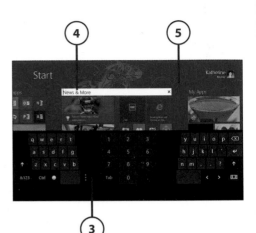

Removing an App from the Start Screen

As soon as you launch Windows 8.1 for the first time, you'll notice that Microsoft has given you a number of apps by default. You might—or might not—want to keep those apps. If you want to remove some of the unnecessary apps, you can do that easily and give yourself a little extra room on the Start screen.

1. Select the app you want to remove by tapping and holding the app tile or right-clicking it.

2. The apps bar appears along the bottom of the Start screen. To unpin the app, so that it is still installed on your computer but simply not visible as an app on the Start screen, tap or click Unpin from Start.

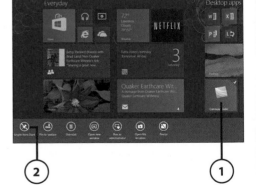

Searching in Windows 8.1

People seem to love Windows 8.1 search. The search capabilities of the operating system have been enhanced so that you can easily find apps, settings, and files—and now, in Windows 8.1, images, videos, and web content—by simply typing. That's it. You don't need to go to a special page; you don't need to choose a special tool. Windows 8.1 is listening to you and as soon as you start typing something on the Start screen, Windows begins searching.

Windows 8.1 adds Bing integration to Search so you can go beyond what search finds on your computer and include web results to whatever you're looking for. Not only is this reach of search comprehensive, but it's also beautiful, including images, video clips, and more.

Finding Something Fast

To search for something you want in Windows 8.1, just type it. You don't need to go anywhere special. You don't have to click this or that. If you're on the Windows Start screen, as soon as you start typing, Windows 8.1 begins searching for what it thinks you want (which you have an opportunity to correct, of course, if you change your mind midstream).

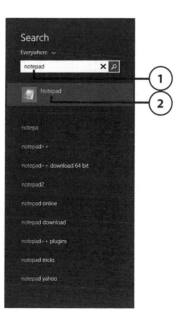

1. On the screen, if your computer or device has a keyboard, type **notepad**.

2. Before you even get to the letter e, Windows 8.1 displays the Search pane with initial search results. If you see the result you want, tap it in the list and Windows 8.1 launches that result.

Using the Virtual Keyboard

If you're using a touch device with no keyboard, swipe in to the left from the right side of the screen to display the Charms bar, tap Search, and tap in the Search box. The onscreen keyboard appears.

Extending Your Search

Above the Search box on the left, you can tap or click the arrow to the right of Everywhere to extend your search. The options list offers you Everywhere, Settings, Files, Web Images, and Web Videos. To change the type of result shown in the results list, click the option you want to apply.

Searching and Finding with Bing

If you want to include as much information as you can in your range of search results, you can easily display the results full-screen and then scroll through to review the results you receive. First, make sure the Search setting is set to Everywhere, and then type what you're searching for. When the preliminary list appears, click or tap the search tool to see the full-screen result; then browse to and tap or click the result you want.

1. On the Windows 8.1 Start screen, type **london**. The Search pane appears, offering a list of results.

2. Tap or click the Search tool. The search results screen appears.

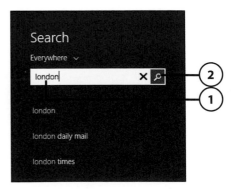

3. Tap or click a file to open it.

4. Scroll to the right to view additional search results.

5. Review the Bing information related to the search.

SEARCHING FROM THE WINDOWS 8.1 DESKTOP

You can search from the Windows 8.1 Desktop by pressing the Windows key or swiping in from the right side of the screen and tapping or clicking the Search charm.

Searching Within an App

When you're working with a particular app, you can use the Charms bar to search for what you're looking for within the program. This works equally well whether you're looking for a tool that is part of the actual app itself or you're looking for something you want the program to find, such as a certain destination in the Maps app.

1. Display the app you want to use.

2. Display the Charms bar.

3. Tap or click Search.

4. Click or tap the arrow to the right of Everywhere. A list of search options appears, displaying the open app at the bottom of the list.

5. Choose the app in which you want to search.

6. Type the word or phrase you want to search for.

7. Tap or click the Search tool.

8. Windows 8.1 displays the search results within the app. Choose a search result that offers the information you need.

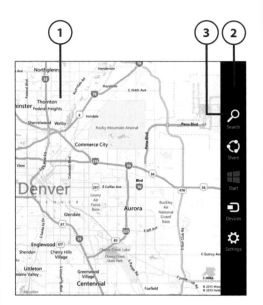

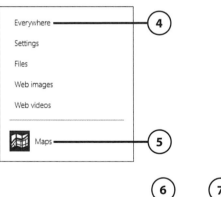

The Windows 8.1 Desktop
provides a familiar backdrop
for traditional programs.

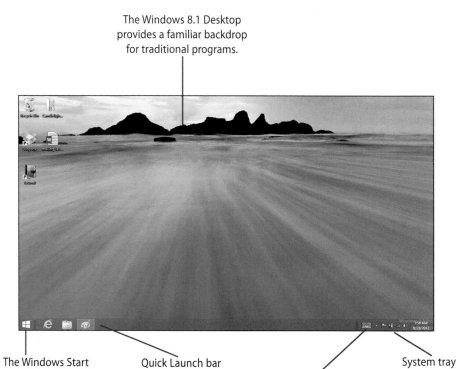

The Windows Start
button takes you back
to the Start screen.

Quick Launch bar

Display Touch Keyboard

System tray

Working with the Desktop

One of the big stories in Windows 8.1 is that now users who aren't fond of the Start screen can bypass it altogether and boot directly to the Windows 8.1 Desktop, which might just remind you of Windows 7. You don't lose anything in terms of flexibility, however, and you still have access to the Windows 8.1 Start screen, thanks to the new Start button Microsoft has positioned in the lower-left corner of the Desktop.

This chapter introduces you to the Desktop and shows you how to launch Windows 8.1 in that direction, if that's your preference. Along the way, you'll learn to work with windows, use jump lists, set up shortcuts, and more.

Moving Between the Desktop and the Start Screen

The first thing you'll need to do when you access and work with the desktop is know how to move from the Start screen to the desktop and back. When you log in to your computer or device, the Windows 8 Start screen appears. You can then display the Windows desktop by tapping or clicking the Desktop tile or by typing *desktop* and tapping or clicking the Desktop app that appears in the search results.

Displaying the Windows 8.1 Desktop

When you first start Windows 8.1, the desktop doesn't get much fanfare. Instead, you'll need to find it—it's a small app tile on the colorful Start screen. Even though the tile is small, the desktop still packs a lot of punch. That's where you'll be working with most of the familiar applications you use every day, like Microsoft Office and other favorite programs.

1. On the Windows 8.1 Start screen, tap or click Desktop.

2. The Windows 8.1 desktop appears. Here you can see any legacy programs you've installed with Windows 8.1, as well as the programs you've pinned to the taskbar.

3. Tap or click an icon to launch a program.

Using the Windows 8.1 Start Button

One of the new additions—to much celebration-—in Windows 8.1 is the new Start button. This button doesn't function in quite the same ways as the Start button we used in Windows 7, but it does take you back to the Start screen and, if right-clicked, gives you access to a menu of tools you can use to manage the use of your computer.

1. Display the Windows 8.1 desktop.

2. Tap or click the Start button. You are returned to the Start screen. As you'll notice, the Start button appears for a moment in the lower-left corner of the Start screen as well, so you can move quickly back to the desktop again by clicking it a second time.

3. Right-click the Start button. A listing of "power user" tools appears.

4. Select the tool you want to use by tapping or clicking it.

Charming Your Way Back to Start

You can also return to the Start screen by displaying the Charms bar and tapping the Start button or by pressing the Windows key on your keyboard.

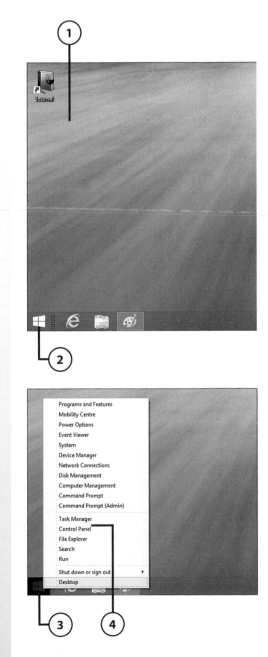

Programs and Features
Mobility Centre
Power Options
Event Viewer
System
Device Manager
Network Connections
Disk Management
Computer Management
Command Prompt
Command Prompt (Admin)
Task Manager
Control Panel
File Explorer
Search
Run
Shut down or sign out
Desktop

Launching to the Windows 8.1 Desktop

You might have heard masses of power users grumbling about the Window Start screen when the new operating system was first released. Many experienced computer users (and some others as well) felt the Windows 8 Start screen wasn't intuitive and made accessing apps more difficult than it needed to be. For this reason, Microsoft included in Windows 8.1 the option of launching directly to the desktop. This lets you avoid the Start screen altogether unless you have a cause to use it.

Setting Windows 8.1 to launch to the desktop is a simple task, and you can undo the operation and return to the Start screen at startup whenever you choose.

Launching Windows 8.1 to the Desktop

When you first tell Windows 8.1 you want to launch straight to the desktop, there are a few extra steps involved in the process, but after you get everything set up, as soon as you enter your password on the Lock screen, the Windows 8.1 desktop meets your ready gaze.

1. Display the Windows 8.1 desktop.

2. Right-click the taskbar.

3. Click or tap Properties. The Taskbar and Navigation Properties dialog box appears.

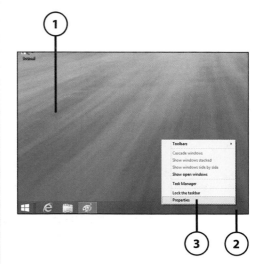

4. Click the Navigation tab.

5. In the Start Screen area, click or tap the Go to the Desktop Instead of Start When I Sign In check box.

6. Click OK. The dialog box closes, and the next time you sign in to Windows 8.1, the desktop will appear.

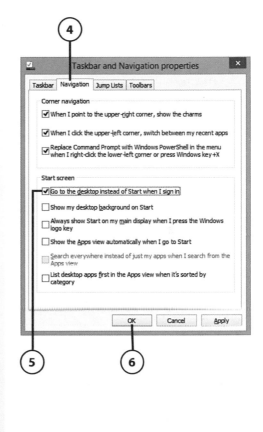

Adding the Desktop Background to the Start Screen

If you want a consistent look and feel for both the desktop and the Start screen, you can have Windows 8.1 use the same background for both. Simply click the Show My Desktop Background on Start check box in the Navigation tab of the Taskbar and Navigation Properties dialog box and click OK. Then whenever you switch from the desktop to the Start screen and back again, you'll see the familiar background wherever you go.

Getting Ready to Work with Programs

Although more and more developers are creating versions of their programs that run on Windows 8.1, there is still a world full of applications that were designed for Windows 7. The good news is that you can run these programs in Windows 8.1. When you launch them, they will open automatically on the Windows 8.1 desktop. You can also create shortcuts that you can place on the desktop so you can run the program by clicking or tapping an icon, or you can pin the app to the Windows 8.1 taskbar, where you can launch it easily.

More About Working with Programs

You'll learn more about downloading, installing, and working with programs in Chapter 7, "Diving in with Apps."

Adding Shortcuts

A shortcut is a program icon
Windows places on your desktop
that gives you a quick way to launch
a program. You can add shortcuts for
your favorite programs so you can
start them right from the Windows 8
desktop. Here's how:

1. Tap or right-click the desktop.

2. Tap or click New.

3. Tap or click Shortcut. The Create
   Shortcut dialog box appears.

4. Click or tap the Browse button.
   The Browse for Files or Folders
   dialog box appears.

5. Navigate to the folder that
   contains the program you want
   to add as a shortcut. Click the
   program.

6. Click OK.

7. In the Create Shortcut dialog box,
   click Next.

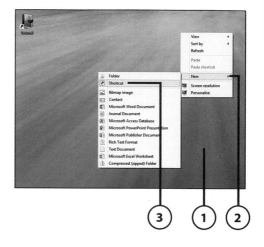

8. Enter a name for the shortcut.

9. Click Finish. The shortcut appears
    on the desktop, and you can
    launch the program by double-
    clicking (or double-tapping) the
    shortcut icon.

Do-Over!

If you decide after you create a
shortcut that you really aren't
going to use it and it's just taking up desktop space, you can
easily delete it. Click the shortcut
icon one time to select it on the
desktop, and then press Delete.
(Tablet users can tap and hold on
the shortcut to open an option
list from which you can delete it.)
Windows 8.1 deletes the shortcut
with no further ado or prompt.
(You can open the Recycle Bin
and drag the shortcut back to
your desktop if you change your
mind and decide you want to
keep it, however.)

Launching File Explorer

If you enjoy keeping your files and
folders organized, you might already
be wondering where to find File
Explorer in Windows 8.1. Because
that program runs only on your
desktop, you first need to display the
Windows 8.1 desktop before you can
start File Explorer.

Create Shortcut

What would you like to name the shortcut?

Type a name for this shortcut:

My Journal

Click Finish to create the shortcut.

Finish   Cancel

8

9

1. On the Windows 8.1 desktop, tap the File Explorer icon in the task-bar.

2. File Explorer appears, offering the familiar three-column layout (familiar, that is, if you used File Explorer in Windows 7), but you'll notice something new. Now File Explorer sports its own ribbon, with tools and settings you can use to manage your files and folders in Windows 8.1.

3. When you're ready, tap or click the Start button to return to the Start screen.

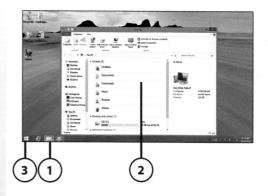

More About File Explorer

Chapter 8, "Organizing Files with File Explorer," tells you all about organizing and working with files and folders in File Explorer.

Tailoring the Taskbar

The desktop taskbar is a place for lots of activity on the Windows 8.1 desktop. By default, you'll find two icons in the Quick Launch area, to the far-left end of the taskbar: Internet Explorer 11 and File Explorer. You can start either of those programs by clicking or tapping those icons. You can also add programs you use often to the desktop taskbar so you can launch them. For example, if you record audio notes regularly, you might want to add Sound Recorder to the taskbar; if you work with illustrations, you could add Windows Paint. Any app you use regularly is a good candidate for the Windows 8.1 desktop.

Adding Apps to the Taskbar on the Desktop

The first step in adding an app to the desktop taskbar is to launch the program you want to add. You can start the program from either the Windows 8.1 Start screen or the desktop.

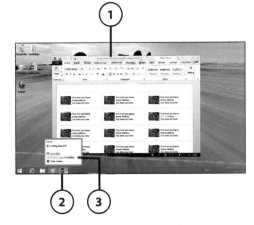

1. Open the desktop app you want to add to the Windows 8.1 desktop taskbar.

2. Right-click the app icon in the taskbar, or tap and hold the icon until a square appears around it. A list of options appears.

3. Tap or click Pin This Program to Taskbar.

Pinning Apps from the Start Screen

You can also tell Windows 8.1 you want to pin an app to the taskbar when you're working on the Start screen. Here's how:

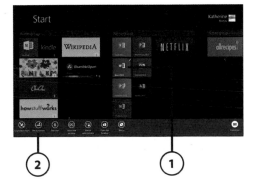

1. On the Start screen, tap and hold or right-click the app you want to add to the taskbar.

2. In the Apps bar, tap or click Pin to Taskbar. The Apps bar closes and when you display the desktop, the new app appears in the taskbar.

Unpinning, After the Fact

If you decide that your taskbar is getting cluttered or you want to remove items you've pinned there, right-click the pinned item (or tap and hold your finger on the item until a square appears around it and then release your touch to display the options list), and select Unpin This Program from Taskbar. Instantly it's gone—like it was never even there.

Using Jump Lists

Jump lists are popular features in Windows 7 that enable you to get right to documents and files you've worked with recently without opening menus or launching new programs. A jump list keeps track of the most recent files you've worked with in a program you've pinned to the taskbar, and you can display the whole list by clicking the icon on the taskbar. You can then click the file you want and move right to it.

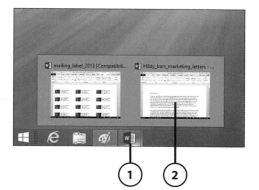

1. Hover the mouse over the program icon in the taskbar.

2. Alternatively, tap the program icon in the taskbar. The files currently open in that program appear above the taskbar.

Jump List Display

If you have only a few files in your jump list, the files will appear as thumbnails; when you have a whole slew of files (the default setting in Jump List properties is 10), you'll see a list of files instead of thumbnails.

KEEPING YOUR JUMP LISTS QUIET

In Windows 8.1, you have additional control over what gets displayed in your jump lists. If you'd rather others who use your computer not be able to see the files you've worked with recently, you can uncheck the Store and Display Recently Opened Items in Jump Lists check box. Here's how to do that.

Right-click the Windows 8.1 desktop taskbar and select Properties. Click the Jump Lists. You'll find the option you want in the Privacy area. Click Store and Display Recently Opened Items in Jump Lists check box to clear the selection. Now click OK to close the dialog box, and you're all set.

Working with Windows on the Windows Desktop

When you work with programs on the Windows 8.1 desktop, they will appear in the type of windows you'll be familiar with if you've used previous versions of Windows. You can open, close, minimize, maximize, arrange, and resize the windows. You'll be able to click or tap the title bar of the window and move it from place to place. And you'll also be able to arrange more than one window on the screen at the same time.

Window Basics

The windows you'll open on the Windows 8.1 desktop have a number of elements in common:

- The title bar displays the name of the program and may display the name of the open file.

- The Minimize, Maximize, and Close buttons control the size of the window. Minimize reduces the window to the taskbar; Maximize opens the window so that it fills the screen; and Close closes the window.

- The Quick Access Toolbar gives you access to commands you might want to use with the program. You can customize the Quick Access Toolbar by clicking the arrow on the right and selecting additional commands from the list.

- Click the Help button to display help information related to the program you are using.

- By default, the Ribbon in File Explorer is hidden, giving you the maximum amount of room to work with libraries, files, and folders. To display the Ribbon, tap the Expand the Ribbon tool.

- Click the Minimize Ribbon tool to reduce the display of the Ribbon so that only the tab names show. When the Ribbon is hidden, the tool changes to Expand the Ribbon.

- The Ribbon tabs offer different sets of tools related to the tasks you're likely to want to perform in the program.

- You can click and drag the window border to resize the window.

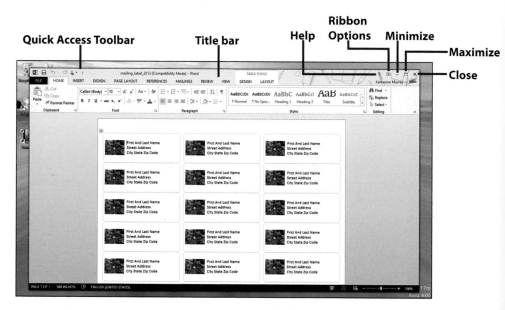

Moving a Window

Moving a window is as simple as tapping or clicking and dragging a window in the direction you want it to go.

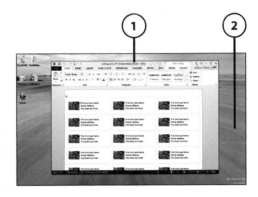

1. Tap and drag—or click and drag—the window's title bar.

2. Drag the window in the direction you want to move it, and release it in the new position.

Resizing a Window

The easiest way to resize a window, from small to large, is to use the Maximize button in the window controls in the upper-right corner of the window. You can also resize a window by positioning the pointer on the window border or corner and dragging in the direction you want to resize the window.

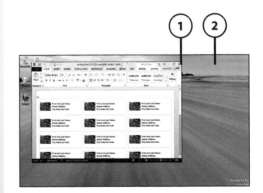

1. Tap or point to a corner or side of the window.

2. Drag the border in the direction you want to resize the window, and release the border (or the mouse button) when the window is the size you want it.

Switching to a Different Window

While you're working on the desktop, you can easily have many windows open on the screen at once. These windows might be program windows or folders of files. If you work with a number of programs open at one time, of course, you need to be able to get to the program you want when you need it. If several windows are open on the screen at once, you can click any part of the window you want to bring to the top, or you can click the taskbar icon of the window you want to view. Alternatively, you can press and hold Alt+Tab to display a pop-up box and then press Tab repeatedly to cycle through open programs. When the window you want is selected, release Alt+Tab and that window opens on your desktop.

Arranging Windows

Another important task when you are working with multiple windows open on the screen at one time is having the ability to arrange the windows the way you want them to appear. If you want to compare two documents, for example, it would be nice to show them side-by-side. You can arrange windows the way you want on the Windows 8.1 desktop.

1. Right-click the taskbar and select Cascade Windows.

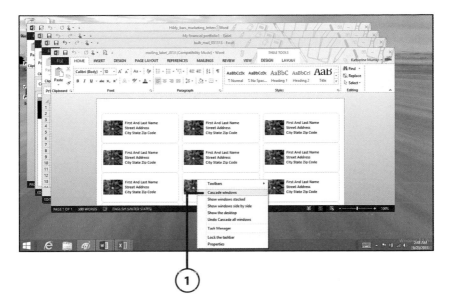

2. Right-click the taskbar and select Show Windows Stacked.

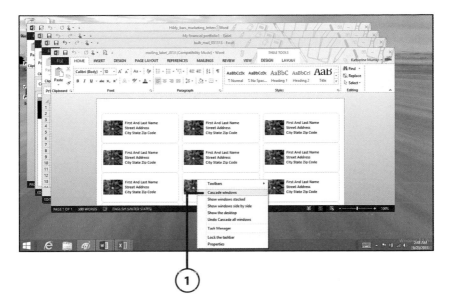

3. Right-click the taskbar and click Show Windows Side By Side.

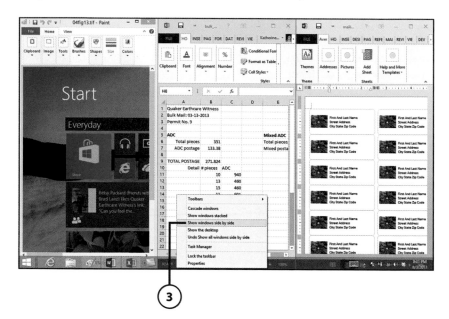

③

SHORTCUT KEYS AND SNAP FOR WINDOW WRANGLING

You can also work with the windows on your desktop without ever taking your hands off the keyboard. Here are the shortcut keys you can use:

- Alt+spacebar displays the shortcut menu for the current window.

- Windows+M minimizes all open windows.

- Windows+E opens your This PC folder in File Explorer.

- Windows+D displays the desktop.

Quick-Changing Windows

You can change the size of a window quickly by double-clicking (or double-tapping) the title bar. If the window was full-screen size (that is, maximized), it returns to its earlier smaller size. If the window is smaller than full screen, double-clicking the title bar maximizes it.

Old-Style Resizing

Sure, all these double-click tricks are fancy and fast. But if you prefer to choose commands from menus, you can display any window's control panel and select the command you want—Restore, Move, Size, Minimize, and Close—from the list of options. You can find the control panel for the window in the upper-left corner; you can't miss it because it resembles a small program icon (in Word, you see a Word icon; in Excel, you see an Excel icon; and so forth).

You can use PC Settings to
personalize the look and feel
of Windows 8.1.

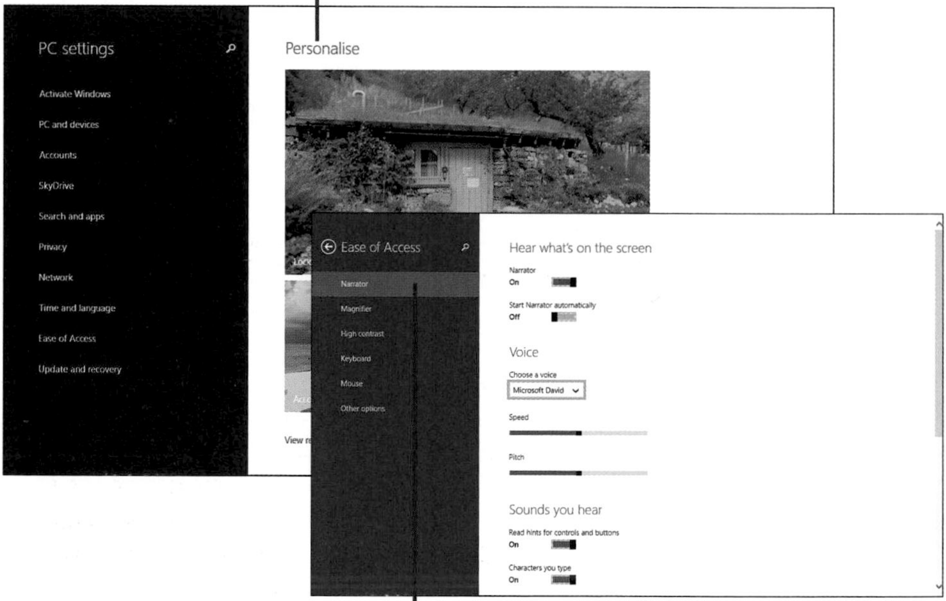

PC settings

Activate Windows

PC and devices

Accounts

SkyDrive

Search and apps

Privacy

Network

Time and language

Ease of Access

Update and recovery

Personalise

← Ease of Access

Narrator

Magnifier

High contrast

Keyboard

Mouse

Other options

View r

Hear what's on the screen

Narrator
On

Start Narrator automatically
Off

Voice

Choose a voice
Microsoft David

Speed

Pitch

Sounds you hear

Read hints for controls and buttons
On

Characters you type
On

The Ease of Access features enable
you to further customize Windows
8.1 to fit your personal work style.

Do you want to make Windows 8.1 your own? In this chapter, you learn to change the way Windows 8.1 looks and acts by doing the following tasks:

→ Personalizing your Lock screen

→ Adding lock screen apps

→ Adjusting the look of Windows 8.1

→ Changing your Windows 8.1 desktop

Making It *Your* Windows 8.1

Today we expect to be able to tweak our technology to reflect our personality and preferences. We choose colors for our smartphone backgrounds; we select specialized ringtones; we apply themes to our browsers; and we create custom playlists for our music selections. Windows 8.1 offers a number of personalization tools you can use to make your computing experience your own. From a custom slide show on the Lock screen to animated Start screen backgrounds to tweaks for gestures and mouse, Windows 8.1 gives you a range of options you can use to personalize your operating system experience.

This chapter shows you how to personalize your Lock screen by adding a custom slide show of your favorite photos and adding Lock screen apps that give you updates on what's happening in your world. You'll also learn how to change the background of both the Start screen and the Desktop (and how to use the same background if that's your preference). You'll also find out how to adjust the responsiveness of your mouse and tweak your touch experience along the way.

Personalizing Your Lock Screen

The Lock screen is the first screen you see when you press Power and your Windows 8.1 PC or device comes to life. The Lock screen shows your profile image and also might show you some notifications—called *badges*—from your email, messaging, and calendar apps. For example, small numbers beside the notifications icons can show you that you have two new email messages, four instant messages, and a meeting invitation to respond to. That's a great time-saver because you can see what needs your attention before you even unlock your computer!

You can personalize the look of your Windows 8.1 Lock screen by changing your profile picture or choosing and changing your own favorite Lock screen apps. Windows 8.1 gives you a number of photos to choose from, but you can use one of your own personal images if you like. What's more, now in Windows 8.1, you can create a custom slide show using your favorite images from different sources, so the Lock screen displays family, friends, and more, even while your computer is locked.

Choosing a New Lock Screen Picture

The picture displayed on your Lock screen initially is a default image selected by Windows 8.1, but you can change that image to show something that has personal meaning for you. You can change your Lock screen picture whenever you like, and you begin with the Settings charm to make the change.

1. On the Windows Start screen, swipe in from the right or move the mouse to the upper- or lower-right corner of the screen to display the Charms bar.

2. Tap or click Settings and the bar expands to display a number of setting icons.

3. Tap or click Change PC Settings. The PC Settings window appears, with the Top Settings shown by default in the initial screen.

4. Click or tap Lock Screen. The Preview screen appears, showing you the picture currently selected for the Lock screen and offering additional pictures (or the option to upload a new one of your own).

5. Tap or click one of the thumbnail pictures below the selected photo if you want to use an image displayed below the selected picture.

6. If you want to use one of your own images for your Lock screen, tap or click Browse. The Files window appears, displaying pictures and folders in your Pictures folder.

7. Click or tap the arrow to the right of This PC. A list of locations appears.

8. Choose the location where the pictures you want to use are stored.

9. Tap or click the photo you want to use. A small check mark appears in the upper-right corner of the image you selected.

10. Tap or click Choose Image. The new image is added to the preview area in the Lock screen settings.

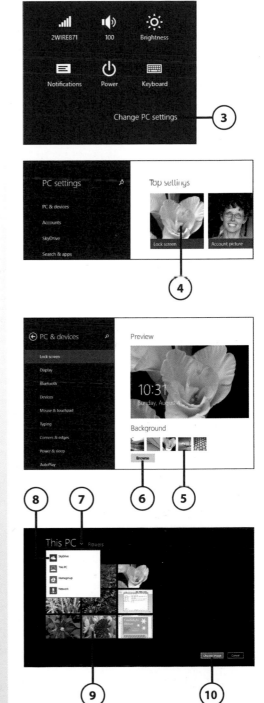

Saving Your Changes—Not

Yes, it's a little hard to get used to, but there's no Save Changes button in the Personalize settings. Windows 8.1 saves your changes as you work, so you don't need to take a specific action to complete the operation. If you're one of those people (like me) who likes to wrap things up neatly, not having a Save button is a little disconcerting, but we'll get used to it (hopefully).

Adding a New Lock Screen Picture On-the-Fly

If you're viewing photos on your computer and see an image you particularly like, you can make that photo your Lock screen image instantly. Here's how to do that:

1. Display the photo you want to use as the Lock screen.

2. Swipe up from the bottom of the screen or right-click to display the photo options.

3. Tap or click Set As.

4. Tap or click Lock Screen. The new photo is applied instantly as your Lock screen image.

More Photo Tips, Please

You learn much more about working with photos in Windows 8.1 in Chapter 11, "Media and More."

Creating a Slide Show for the Lock Screen

One of the new features in Windows 8.1 is the ability to create and play a slide show on the Lock screen. This is a nice background feature that can help add some ambiance to your work when you're not actively using your tablet or PC. When you're ready to start working, you can tap or click or press a key on the keyboard, and Windows 8.1 scrolls the slide show away and displays your login information so you can enter your password or PIN and get to work. Here's how to create a slide show for your Lock screen:

1. In the PC Settings screen, tap Lock Screen to display the Lock screen settings.

2. In the Slide Show area, slide the Play a Slide Show on the Lock Screen control to On.

3. If you want Windows 8.1 to display the slide show even when your computer or device is not plugged in, slide the Play a Slide Show When Using Battery Power to On.

4. Scroll down to reveal more options.

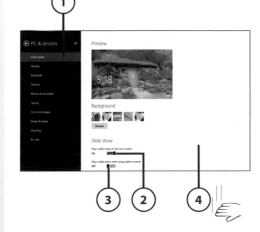

5. If you want Windows 8.1 to use photos from the Pictures folder on your PC or device, tap or click Pictures.

6. If you want to choose a folder in another location (such as SkyDrive or a social media account), click or tap Add a Folder.

7. Click the down-arrow and select the location where the folder is stored.

8. Click or tap the folder you want to use. The folder opens to display the contents of the folder.

9. Select multiple folders, if you like, by swiping down on a folder or right-clicking it, and then swiping or right-clicking additional folders. Tap or click Select All in the App Options bar if you want to choose all folders.

10. If you want to let Windows 8.1 select the slide show picture for you, you can leave the Let Windows Choose Pictures for My Slide Show option set to On. If you want to make the selection, drag the slider to Off.

11. Click or tap the down-arrow and select when you want the slide show to begin.

12. Tap or click the down-arrow and select when you want to turn off the slide show.

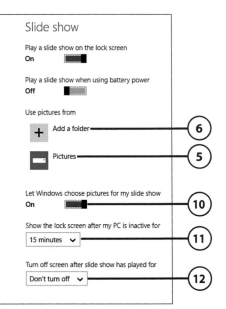

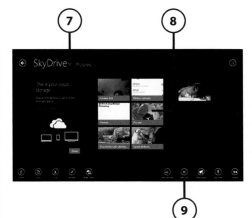

Creating Themed Slide Shows

You can easily create different slide shows for your Lock screen that suit your different moods or locations. For example, if you want to display a work-related slide show during work hours (perhaps with photos of your latest projects or staff activities) and family images at home, you can store the different photos in folders named, appropriately, Work and Home; then you can choose the folder you want to use for the slide show on-the-fly. This enables you to create as many slide shows as you like, and all you have to do is choose the folder with the images you want to show. Nice.

Changing Your Account Picture

Your account picture appears—in a tiny size—in the upper-right corner of your Windows Start screen. You'll also see it when you swipe up on your Lock screen. Similar to your profile picture in your favorite social media account, your account picture is your own personal expression. You can change your account picture in Windows 8.1 as often as you like by switching it out in your PC Settings. Begin by displaying the Charms bar, tapping or clicking Settings, and selecting Change PC Settings.

1. In the Top Settings area, tap or click Account Picture.

2. To choose a new picture from the files on your computer, tap or click Browse.

3. In the Files screen, tap or click the photo you want to use.

4. Tap or click Choose Image; Windows 8.1 adds it to your Account Picture preview. Any other pictures you've added previously are also still available in the Account Picture area so you can select them at any time.

5. If you want to add a picture using the camera on your laptop or tablet, tap or click Camera.

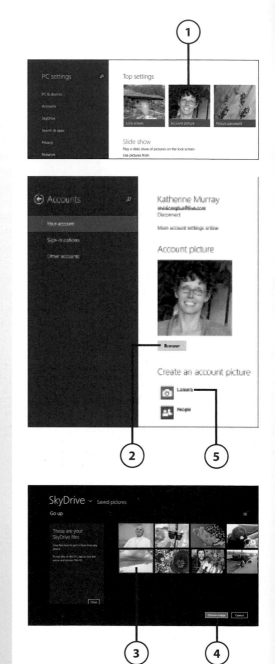

6. When the picture you want to capture is displayed, tap or click anywhere on the screen to take the photo.

Fewer Choices, Please

If you go through a whole slew of possible account picture choices and aren't particularly happy with any of them, you can remove the ones that appear as thumbnails beneath your chosen picture in the Account Picture screen. Simply right-click the picture and select Clear History. Windows wipes away the images you've added like they were never there.

7. Windows 8 displays the picture in a preview screen. Click the cropping handles to adjust what remains visible in the picture.

8. When the picture is displayed the way you want it to appear, tap or click OK.

9. You can also choose an account picture you've used on a social media site. Click or tap People and browse to select the image you want to use.

Retaking a Photo

If you want to replace the photo you just captured, tap or click Retake and repeat steps 6–8. Windows 8.1 then substitutes the new webcam photo for your Account Picture in the Personalize settings.

Where Are These Things Stored?

If you go to the trouble of creating and saving different account pictures, are they stored somewhere so that you can switch them as the fancy strikes you? Yes, thankfully, all the images you use as account pictures—whether you browse for them or capture them using your webcam—are stored in an Account Pictures folder. To see all the images that are available to use as account pictures, display the Top settings, tap or click Account Picture, and select Browse. You can then change the account picture by selecting the image you want to use and tapping or clicking the Choose Image button.

Adding Lock Screen Apps

Lock screen apps appear on your Lock screen and give you up-to-date notifications about your various apps, such as how many email messages and instant messages you need to respond to. Other Lock screen apps are available as well. You can change the number and selection of the Lock screen apps on the PC & Devices screen.

1. Display the PC Settings screen and tap or click PC & Devices. Choose Lock Screen.

2. Scroll down to the Lock Screen Apps area.

3. Tap or click a + in the apps area. The Choose an App pop-up window appears.

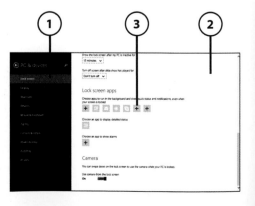

4. Tap or click the app you want to add as a badge on your Lock screen. Windows 8.1 will display the information related to that app on the Lock screen.

Lock Screen Apps Show Up Other Places, Too

Lock screen apps also control the tiny items that show up as notifications on the live tiles on your Windows Start screen. For example, when you notice that your Messaging app tile suddenly shows 3 in the lower corner (when just a minute ago it didn't show any number at all), that's because the Lock Screen app received and is displaying an update.

Choose an app

Alarms

Calendar ——————————— **4**

Mail

Skype

>>>Go Further

TAKING PHOTOS WITH A LOCKED PC

Windows 8.1 doesn't want to cramp your style if you like to take photos with your tablet while you're on the road. What's more, Windows doesn't want to squelch your creative eye by requiring that you log in before you can fire up your camera. To keep things simple, you can now take photos with your Windows 8.1 device, right from the Lock screen.

You'll find the options you need to set this up in the PC & Devices screen. On the Lock screen tab, scroll down to Camera and slide the Use Camera from the Lock Screen control to On. Now when you want to take a picture while your Lock screen appears, simply swipe down on the Lock screen, and Windows 8.1 grabs the photo for you. Simple.

Adjusting the Look of Windows 8.1

Because you might be spending a lot of time with the Windows 8.1 Start screen, you're probably interested in personalizing that display as well. Windows 8.1 now includes a wide range of themes you can choose, including a few themes that actually have animated backgrounds.

As much as you might love the color schemes and enjoy the fluid way Windows moves, you might have trouble making out the small words on the tiles or focusing on things as they pass (not saying you need to have your eyes checked or anything, *ahem*). There's good news—Windows 8.1 has Ease of Access options that can make your computing experience a bit easier, and I show you how to work with them in this section.

Tweaking Start

To change the Start screen's color, start off by displaying the Windows 8.1 Charms bar, tapping or clicking Settings, and choosing Change PC Settings.

1. Display the Charms and select Settings.

2. In the Settings panel, tap Personalize. A gallery of themes appears, along with colors you can choose to accent the theme.

3. Tap or click the theme you want to apply to the background. The Start screen changes to reflect your selection.

4. In the Background color control, drag the color selector to a new color to see the effect of the change.

5. In the Accent color area, drag the color selector to the hue you want.

Click a Color, Too

When you drag the color slider to a color you want (for the Background or Accent colors), you can narrow the color choice still further if you like. Click the color in the gallery above the slider to experiment with different effects. When you find the color you want, leave it selected.

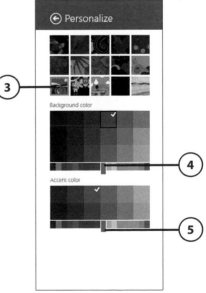

>>> Go Further

BEFORE YOU CHANGE THINGS...

If you like the color you've already got on the Windows Start screen, make a mental note of which color scheme is selected before you change it to something else. The first time I changed the color configuration in Windows 8.1, I wasn't completely happy with the new selection, and after I changed the color back, I wasn't 100% sure I'd chosen the color scheme I had before. (This is one of those places where having a Cancel button would be nice.)

Contrast Makes the Heart Grow Fonder

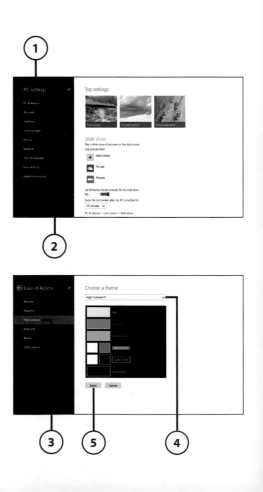

Windows 8.1 includes a High Contrast option so that you can display Windows in a way that heightens the contrast on the screen, which can make things easier to read if you're struggling with things as they are.

1. Display the PC Settings screen (tap the Settings charm and select Change PC Settings).

2. Tap or click Ease of Access on the left side of the screen.

3. Click or tap High Contrast.

4. Choose a theme from the list box at the top of the screen. When you select a theme, Windows 8.1 shows you the effects of the contrast theme you've selected.

5. Click Apply to add the high contrast theme to Windows 8.1.

Magnifying Your Display

Another way you can enhance the readability of your Windows 8.1 screen involves magnifying the entire screen. You can do this by changing another of the Ease of Access settings.

1. Tap or click Magnifier in the Ease of Access window.

2. On the right side of the screen, drag the slider in the Magnifier setting from Off to On.

3. Your screen magnifies instantly, and you can navigate as normal (but you might need to do a lot more scrolling). Click the Magnifying Glass tool to display the Magnifier toolbar.

4. Use the - and + buttons to enlarge or reduce the magnification of the screen.

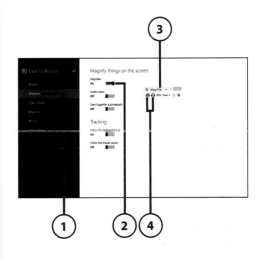

Changing the Time

It's likely that the first time you log in to your new Windows computer (or the first time you fire up Windows 8.1 on your old computer), the program will ask you to verify or choose your time zone. But if necessary, you can let Windows know what time it is where you are so that you're in sync no matter who you're chatting with online and where in the world they might be. (This becomes especially important if you're a traveler and you take your Windows computer or device on the road with you.) Having the time set to your local time is also helpful when you are scheduling calls and online meetings with others who might be in different time zones.

1. Display the PC Settings window and tap or click Time & Language. The Time & Language screen appears.

2. If necessary, slide the Set Time Automatically feature to On.

3. In the Time Zone area, tap or click the time zone arrow to display a list of available time zones and select the zone you want to use.

4. Leave the Adjust Clock for Daylight Saving Time Automatically turned on if you want the time to be adjusted for you when Daylight Saving Time changes.

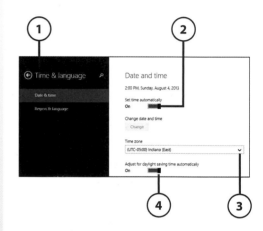

Changing Your Windows 8.1 Desktop

Now that you know how to change the look of the Start screen, you also might want to tweak the look of your Windows 8.1 desktop. Depending on the type of computer you purchased and the choices of the manufacturer, you could have a different customized desktop (for example, showing your computer manufacturer's logo in addition to the traditional Windows color scheme). You can modify the background, and choose some great new looks, with other themes and backgrounds available for your desktop in Windows 8.1.

Coordinating the Desktop and the Start Screen

Now in Windows 8.1, you can give both the Desktop and the Start screen the same background, which can help the switch between Start and Desktop seem less jarring. Right-click or tap and hold the taskbar on the Desktop, and then select Properties. Click or tap the Navigation tab, and click or tap to select the Show My Desktop Background on Start check box. Click or tap OK to save your changes, and the new background is applied to your Start screen as well as the Desktop.

Selecting a New Desktop Background

Windows 8.1 offers you a number of choices for your background image. You can select a single image or multiple images that display at increments you set, like a slide show.

1. Display the Desktop and right-click (or tap and hold and then release) a blank area on the desktop. A list of options appears.

2. Click or tap Personalize.

3. Click or tap Desktop Background. The Desktop Background window appears.

4. Click the Picture Location arrow to select the choices for backgrounds displayed in the Background window. If you select Pictures Library, you can click Browse to choose the folder containing the images you want to use.

5. Drag the scrollbar to view all the choices in the display window.

6. Click at least three background images by clicking the check box in the upper-left corner of the image.

7. Click the Picture Position arrow and choose whether you want the image to fill the screen, fit the screen width, stretch, tile, or center.

8. Click the Change Picture Every arrow and select how often you want pictures to change on the desktop. Your choices range from

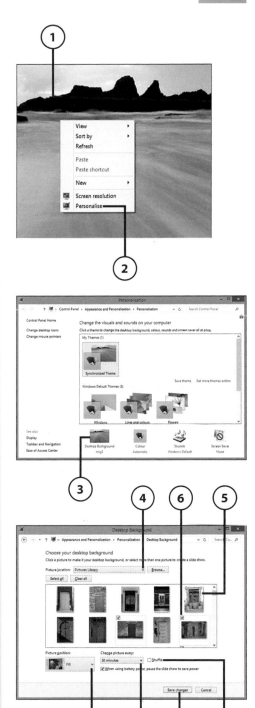

changing every 10 seconds (which is fast!) to changing once a day.

9. Click the Shuffle check box if you want the order of the images to be shuffled so they appear in different orders.

10. Click Save Changes.

Going Green with Your Slide Show

By default, Windows 8.1 is set to pause the slide show if your laptop or device is running on battery power. If you want the slide show to continue whether your computer is plugged in or not, you can uncheck the When Using Battery Power, Pause the Slide Show to Save Power check box.

>>>Go Further

CHOOSING A DESKTOP THEME

A theme for your Windows 8.1 desktop coordinates the desktop background, color scheme, sounds, and screensaver. You can choose the theme by displaying the desktop, right-clicking or tapping and holding and then selecting Personalize, and then clicking the theme you want in the My Themes area of the Personalization dialog box.

If you don't see a theme that suits you, click the Get More Themes Online link. You'll find a variety of theme categories—new themes, animals, art, automotive, branded themes, games, holidays and seasons, movies, nature, and places and landscapes—to view a collection of themes related to the various topics. To find out more about a specific theme, click the Details link. To download a theme you like, click the Download link just beneath it and click Open in the notification bar that appears at the bottom of the screen. The theme is stored in your My Themes area of the Personalization window in the Control Panel.

Picture passwords give you a unique and colorful way to safeguard your computer.

Windows 8.1 offers several different ways to protect your sign-in information.

This chapter shows you how to keep your PC safe by focusing on the following tasks:

→ Customizing your login
→ Working with the Action Center
→ Using Windows Defender
→ Turning on your Windows Firewall
→ Working with user accounts
→ Maintaining your privacy

Securing Your Computer

As a natural part of software evolution, Windows should be getting safer and more secure with each new release. Chris Hallum, senior product manager at Microsoft, says this is so, adding that "Windows 7 is 6 times more likely to get infected than Windows 8, and Windows XP is 21 times more likely to be exploited." (See www.techradar.com/us/news/software/operating-systems/windows-8-1-security-what-s-been-improved-1156705.)

Windows 8.1 is the most secure Windows yet, offering encryption, better malware protection, and a range of tools on the technical end with a focus on additional security for enterprises. But the security features in the version of Windows 8.1 you're using on your computers and devices is nothing to sneeze at. Thanks to improvements in Defender and a variety of ways you can guard your privacy and set up your security features, Windows 8.1 intends to keep your data *your* data and safeguard your computer against attack.

New PCs—Security *Before* Startup
In Windows 8.1, PCs that are built on Unified Extensible Firmware Interface (UEFI) firmware can take advantage of enhanced security features like Secure Boot, which does a scan and ensures system elements are okay before Windows 8.1 even boots on your system. If you'd like to learn more about UEFI, you should check out http://www.uefi.org.

Customizing Your Login

We've worked with (and tweaked) the Windows 8.1 Lock screen, which enables you to add your own picture or slide show and display the Lock screen apps you care most about, so you can get the information you want before you even log in. In addition to customizing the Lock screen, you can tweak your login procedure so that Windows 8.1 uses the type of authentication you choose. For example, instead of a regular alphanumeric password, you might want to use a picture password or create a new login PIN for your machine.

Changing a Password

By default, Windows 8.1 asks you to log in with your Windows Live ID and password. You can, however, change your password at any time or choose different types of passwords (for example, a picture password or a PIN logon) to help with authentication.

1. On the Start screen, swipe or click to display the Charms bar.

2. Tap or click Settings.

3. Tap or click Change PC Settings; the PC Settings window appears.

4. Tap or click Accounts on the left side of the screen.

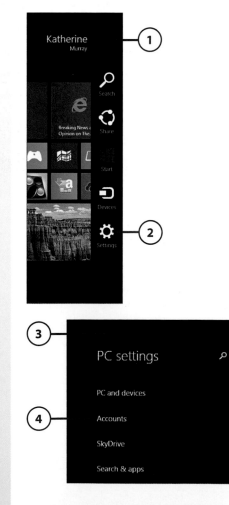

5. Tap or click Sign-In Options.

6. In the Password area, click or tap Change. You will first be prompted to enter your Microsoft Account password. After you enter it, the Change Password screen appears.

7. In the Change Your Password screen, tap or click in the Old Password box and type your old password.

8. Tap or click to move the insertion point to the New Password box, and enter a new password.

9. Retype the new password in the Re-Enter Password box.

10. Tap or click Next. Windows 8.1 lets you know that you've successfully changed your password, and you can click Finish to return to the PC Settings window.

Account Trouble?

If you have forgotten the password you used with your Microsoft Account, you can still change your password online. Click the Forgot Your Password? link, and Windows 8.1 displays a link you can click to go online and resolve the problem.

What Makes a Strong Password?

A strong password is at least eight characters long and doesn't include any recognizable words or number sequences. What's more, you should vary the capitalization of letters, mixing the upper- and lowercase letters. Windows 8.1 remembers your password as case sensitive, which means that 62GoT38 is a different password from 62gOt38.

Creating a Picture Password

Windows 8.1 also gives you the option of setting a picture password. This type of password gives you a unique new way to set up security for your touch-based computer or monitor. You use one of your own pictures and a specific gesture that you trace on the picture to let Windows 8.1 know it's really you logging in to your computer. For example, you might use your finger or mouse pointer to trace a shape on the photo and then draw a line to the lower-right corner. Windows records this gesture, and when you log in using your picture password, any gesture other than the one you recorded won't unlock your computer. Here are the steps to add a picture password:

1. In the PC Settings window, tap or click Picture Password in the Top Settings area.

2. In the Picture Password area, tap or click Add. Select Create a Picture Password. Windows prompts you to enter your current password.

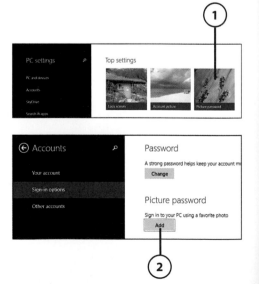

3. Type your current password.

4. Click or tap OK. The Welcome to Picture Password window appears, giving you instructions about the process of creating a picture password.

5. Tap or click Choose Picture.

6. Tap or click the picture you want to use. A small check mark appears in the upper-right corner of the image.

7. Click or tap Open.

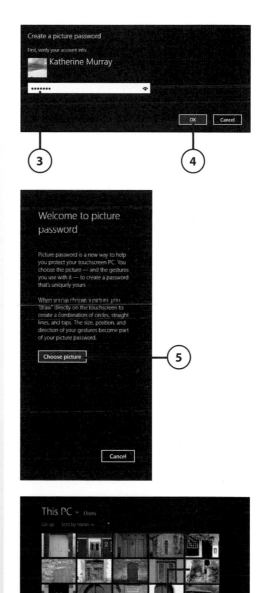

8. If you want to adjust the picture, drag it to the right or left, up or down.

9. Tap or click Use This Picture.

10. If you want to choose a different image instead, tap or click Choose New Picture and repeat steps 5–7.

11. Using your finger or mouse, draw three gestures on the picture. For a moment after you draw on the screen, an arrow shows how Windows recorded the movement. When prompted, repeat the gestures. If you don't make exactly the same gestures, Windows will prompt you to try again.

Starting Over

If you don't like the gesture you've used, you can tap or click Start Over to create new gestures.

12. After you draw the gestures correctly, Windows displays a Congratulations message. Tap or click Finish to save the picture password.

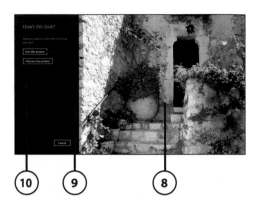

It's Not All Good

THE FUSSINESS OF PICTURE PASSWORDS

One thing you're likely to discover quickly: Picture passwords are very particular. Windows 8.1 might not record your gesture exactly as you think you entered it. If you draw an arc on the screen, Windows may close it to create a circle. Or the line you purposely skewed might show up straight. Use the Try Again option to display the gestures Windows 8.1 is expecting.

It can also help to use a photo that has very definite patterns or lines you can follow and remember easily. Too many curves or too much abstraction can leave you wondering about the specific gestures you need to enter.

Removing a Picture Password

As you can see, using a picture password is great if you want to ensure that you have very personalized security on your computer so that others (who might know your password) won't be able to log in as you. The downside is that the picture password is very particular and specific—so it might be hard for even you to remember!

If you want to remove your picture password, display PC Settings (by tapping or clicking Change PC Settings in the options available when you select the Settings charm) and click Users. Click or tap the Remove button that now appears to the right of the Change Picture Password button to delete the picture password you added.

Creating a PIN Logon

Chances are good that you're familiar with using PINs in other areas of your life. A PIN can give you a quick way to enter a kind of password—you might use a PIN for your ATM card or your credit card account. Similarly, Windows 8.1 enables you to create a four-digit PIN to use when you log in to Windows 8.1.

Begin by displaying the PC Settings screen. Display the Charms bar and select Settings; then tap or click Change PC Settings.

1. Tap or click Accounts to display your account login options.

2. Tap or click Sign-In Options.

3. In the PIN area, tap or click Change.

4. Windows 8.1 prompts you to enter your current password. Tap or click in the box and type the password.

5. Click or tap OK. The Create a PIN screen appears.

Nothing Fancy, Bub

When you create a PIN, Windows 8.1 insists you use only numbers. This means no alphabetic characters, punctuation symbols, or spaces.

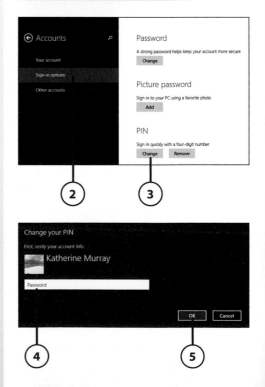

6. Type the four numbers you want to use as your PIN.

7. Tap or click in the Confirm PIN box and retype the numbers you entered.

8. Click or tap Finish. Windows 8.1 saves your PIN; the next time you log in, you can enter the PIN instead of your password. You'll notice that Windows displays the Start screen immediately, even before you press Enter!

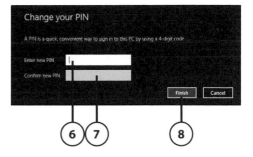

Removing a PIN

If you decide you want to remove your PIN later, you can display the Sign-In Options tab of the Accounts screen again and click Remove in the PIN area. You can, of course, also change the PIN you created by clicking Change and entering and saving a new PIN.

>>>Go Further

HALT! ENTER YOUR PASSWORD!

Some people aren't crazy about the extra step of having to enter their password each time they wake Windows 8.1 from a short nap. You can actually disable this setting—if you're absolutely sure you're not putting your computer or device at risk.

Display the PC Settings screen and tap Accounts. Tap or click the Sign-In Options tab and in the Password Policy area, tap or click Change. Windows 8.1 makes the change automatically, but the operating system displays the following warning: "Anyone will be able to access this PC without a password, no matter who's signed in. This isn't recommended if you use this PC in public."

So if that warning doesn't shake you up and you want to go ahead and change the setting, click or tap OK. The setting on the Sign-In Options changes to Any User Who Has a Password Doesn't Need to Enter It When Waking This PC. (Yes, it's a bit wordy, but it works.)

Working with the Action Center

The Action Center was introduced in Windows 7 to display, in one place, the information you need about any updates your computer needs for both security and regular maintenance purposes. For example, if your antivirus program expires, the Action Center lets you know so you can renew your subscription or find another antivirus program.

The Action Center is alive and well in Windows 8.1. You can use the Action Center to review the status of your system security and to set alerts so you'll know when something important comes up. What's more, you can customize the information in the Action Center so it displays just what you want to see when an alert is in order.

Reviewing Your System Status

You can easily see which security tools are in place on your computer, change settings, and update your software in the Action Center. You can find all the tools you need in the System and Security page of the Control Panel, but you can get to it from the Windows 8.1 Start screen. Here's how:

1. On the Start screen, type **action center**. The Search pane opens, displaying the Action Center tool at the top.

2. Tap or click Action Center.

3. In the Action Center dialog box, review any messages that are displayed. The tag color to the left of the issue indicates the urgency of the issue—yellow warns you that the item should be resolved eventually; red indicates that your attention is needed immediately.

4. Click a link to get more information about the topic. The link might enable you to change settings or view more information about the displayed issue.

5. Click the button that is provided on issues you need to resolve. The name of the button and the task performed will vary depending on what Windows 8.1 is prompting you to do.

6. Click the down-arrow to display additional security settings and make changes as needed.

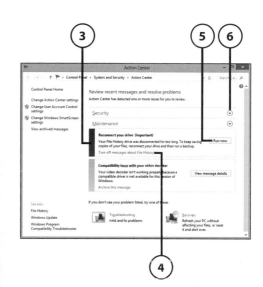

Archiving Messages

After you open and review a message displayed in the Action Center, Windows 8.1 archives the message and removes it from the alert list. To see old Action Center messages, click or tap View Archived Messages in the left side of the Action Center dialog box. To review an archived message, double-click (or double-tap) it. When you're finished viewing archived messages, click OK.

WHY WORRY ABOUT USER ACCOUNT CONTROL?

It's not unusual today when you're surfing the Web to encounter websites and online programs that want to make changes to your computer. Some of these downloads are legitimate—perhaps you need the latest version of Microsoft Silverlight or Adobe Flash to play a movie trailer. But some programs are not so well-intentioned, and these are the ones you need User Account Control to block.

User Account Control lets you easily find out when a program wants to make a change to your computer. You can set up User Account Control so you'll be notified when a program tries to change your system settings. (It's set to do this by default.) Windows 8.1 offers four settings—ranging from Always Notify to Never Notify—and you can easily change the settings by clicking Change User Account Control Settings in the left panel of the Control Panel. Although User Account Control prompts can be annoying, before you disable them, remember that they're there for your protection.

Changing Action Center Alerts

Each Action Center message includes a link that gives you the next step to follow as you deal with the issue. You can choose to turn off messages about that particular issue, archive the message, or ignore the message. You can change which issues you receive alerts for so that you are notified about only the ones you want to see.

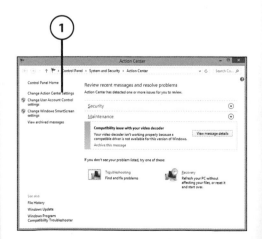

1. In the Action Center, click Change Action Center Settings.

2. Click to uncheck any security item you don't want Windows 8.1 to check for.

3. Click to uncheck any maintenance messages you don't want Windows 8.1 to display.

4. Click OK.

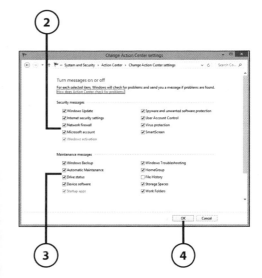

Choice—It's Your Prerogative

Of course, you can change the items Windows 8.1 checks for and the messages you receive at any time. If you turn off an item and then get concerned that maybe you need it after all, simply go to the Action Center, click Change Action Center Settings again, and click to check any unmarked boxes of items you want to add. Click OK to save your settings.

Out of Sight, Out of Mind

Although being alerted for every little thing can be annoying, unless you have a specific reason for turning off an alert for example, Windows 8.1 doesn't recognize the antivirus program you're using on your PC and keeps telling you there's no antivirus program installed—the best practice is to leave all the alerts turned on.

Deciding What to Do with Unrecognized Apps

Windows SmartScreen is a utility within Action Center that keeps an eye on your PC or device and alerts you before Windows 8.1 runs any unrecognized apps or files you've downloaded from the Web. By default, Windows SmartScreen displays a warning before running an unrecognized app. You can change Windows SmartScreen settings if you want to, either to turn off the feature (not a good idea) or to require that administrator approval be given before an unrecognized app can be run.

1. In the Action Center, click Change Windows SmartScreen Settings.

2. Click the new setting you want to apply.

3. Click OK.

Action Center

Control Panel ▸ System and Security ▸ Action Center

Control Panel Home

Change Action Center settings
Change User Account Control settings
Change Windows SmartScreen settings
View archived messages

Review recent messages and resolve problems
No issues have been detected by Action Center.

Security

Maintenance

If you don't see your problem listed, try one of these:

Troubleshooting
Find and fix problems

Recovery
Refresh your PC without affecting your files, or reset it and start over.

See also
File History
Windows Update
Windows Program Compatibility Troubleshooter

1

Windows SmartScreen

What do you want to do with unrecognized apps?

Windows SmartScreen can help keep your PC safer by warning you before running unrecognized apps and files downloaded from the Internet.

○ Get administrator approval before running an unrecognized app from the Internet (recommended)

● Warn before running an unrecognized app, but don't require administrator approval

○ Don't do anything (turn off Windows SmartScreen)

OK   Cancel

Some info is sent to Microsoft about files and apps you run on this PC.
Privacy statement

2   **3**

Using Windows Defender

Windows Defender is an anti-spyware utility that is already installed on your Windows 8.1 PC. Spyware is software that can download itself to your computer without your knowing it, and the makers of the spyware can then find out about your usage habits—or worse, get access to your important files and data. When you have Windows Defender turned on (and it should be on by default), the program runs automatically in the background as you use your computer, blocking any attempts by spyware to download files to your computer and notifying you when programs try to change your Windows settings.

You can use Windows Defender to scan your system regularly and remove any suspicious files that have been added to your computer without your knowledge. Windows Defender in Windows 8.1 includes a network monitoring feature that helps computers on a network detect and stop malware.

Scanning Your PC with Windows Defender

Windows Defender is designed to scan your system every so often—at increments you choose—but you can also choose to do a scan of your PC whenever you like. You might want to do this, for example, if your system is running slowly or you are concerned about your computer's security. You can have Windows Defender scan your PC to make sure no worrisome files have snuck in under your radar.

1. On the Start screen, type **defender**. The Search pane appears, showing Windows Defender as the first result.

2. Tap or click Windows Defender.

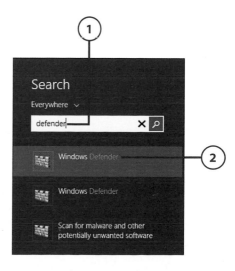

3. Choose the option you want for the type of scan you want Windows Defender to perform.

4. Tap or click the Scan Now button.

Updating Your Definitions

Windows Defender uses what's known as a definitions file to make sure it's checking for the latest viruses and spyware. Defender automatically updates the file, but you can also click or tap the Update tab in the Windows Defender dialog box and then tap or click the Update button to search for updates to the definitions file.

5. After the scan completes, click the History tab to see the scan findings.

6. You can choose the action you want to take related to found items; for example, click Remove All to delete all potentially harmful results.

7. Click the Close box to exit Defender.

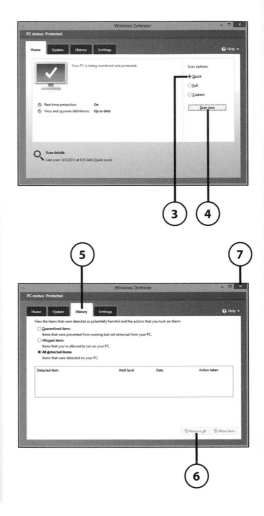

Scanning Styles in Windows Defender	
Type of Scan	**Description**
Quick Scan	Windows Defender checks all files that have been downloaded to your computer since the date of the last scan.
Full Scan	Windows Defender checks all files on all drives and folders in your computer.
Custom Scan	You can choose the drives and folders you want Windows Defender to check.

It's Not All Good

CAN'T WE ALL JUST GET ALONG?

One of the challenges of working with antivirus, spyware, and malware protection programs is that they don't play nicely together. As you can imagine, they are suspicious of everyone; that's their job.

This means that if you have installed another type of antivirus or spyware program, such as Lavasoft's Ad-Aware, Windows Defender might be disabled. Or even when you download and install Microsoft Security Essentials (which includes all the basics of Windows Defender but adds a malware checker too), Windows Defender is turned off so that the other program is turned on.

If you'd rather have Windows Defender operating, you might need to uninstall the other antivirus or spyware software before you can activate Windows Defender. Yes, it's a hassle, but it's one of the prices we pay for secure systems that don't crash every few minutes.

Turning on Your Windows Firewall

A firewall checks all the information coming to your computer from the Internet or from a network to which you might be connected to see whether the sender is a trusted contact and the information can be considered safe for your computer. If any suspicious information is found, your Windows Firewall alerts you so that you can allow or block the sender based on whether you think it should be allowed through the firewall.

Activating the Firewall

Chances are that Windows Firewall is already turned on by default on your computer. You can, however, check the settings and turn on the utility if necessary.

1. On the Start screen, type **firewall**.

2. Tap or click Windows Firewall.

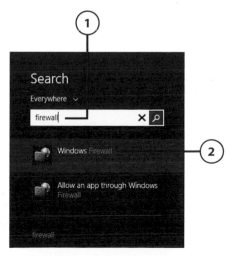

3. Check the Windows Firewall state to make sure your firewall is on.

4. Review the settings in the Private Networks area.

5. Click the Guest or Public Networks arrow to see settings saved for networks in public places such as coffee shops or libraries.

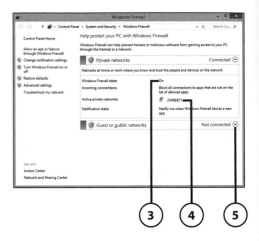

Changing Firewall Settings

When Windows Firewall is active, you are prompted each time a program tries to make changes on your computer if the sender is not on your trusted contacts list. You can change the settings for Windows Firewall so that you receive different alerts.

1. In the left side of the Windows Firewall dialog box, click Change Notification Settings (not pictured).

2. In the Private network area, you can choose whether you want to block incoming connections or be notified when Windows Firewall blocks an app. You can also choose to turn off Windows Firewall for your private network, but that's not recommended.

3. In the Public network settings, you can make the same choices—block everything or get notified about the programs Windows Firewall blocks—for your public network.

4. Click OK to save your changes.

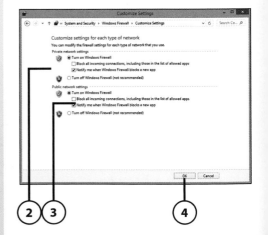

Working with User Accounts

If you share your Windows 8.1 PC with others in your household, it's a good idea to create separate user accounts for each person who uses your computer. This helps you keep your files and programs straight, set the permissions and color schemes you want, use your own passwords, and limit the access others have to your personal information.

You can set user accounts with different privileges (for example, you might want to set up different accounts for your children and use parental controls to make sure they are online only during the hours it's okay with you). You can easily change and customize any user accounts you create at any time.

Add a User

Individual users can have their own user account so that specific preferences, histories, favorites, and more can be kept with that account. To add a new user, start with the PC Settings screen. Display it by choosing the Settings charm and tapping or clicking Change PC Settings.

1. Tap or click Accounts in the PC Settings screen. The Accounts screen appears.

2. Click or tap Other Accounts.

3. Tap or click the + to the left of Add a User.

4. The Add a User window appears. Enter the person's email address.

5. Click Next.

6. If the account you're creating is for a child, click the check box beneath the new user's profile picture placeholder to turn on Family Safety settings.

7. Click Finish. Windows 8.1 tells you to make sure the person knows he needs to be connected to the Internet the first time he logs in.

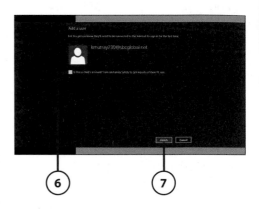

AN ACCOUNT BY ANY OTHER NAME

>>>Go Further

When you add a new user, you'll have the choice to sign the person up using her Microsoft Account or sign up without a Microsoft account. The difference here is that when a person signs in using a Microsoft account, all system preferences—including things like notification settings, color schemes, and more—are available on all the Windows 8.1 computers that person uses when she logs in with her account. Using a Microsoft account also enables users to download apps from the Windows Store and save content to the cloud using SkyDrive. If the new user doesn't sign in with a Microsoft account, settings and preferences are stored only on the local machine.

Changing User Account Settings

You might want to change some of the settings for your account or the user account you've created for others. You can easily change the account name and picture, set other account controls, or even delete accounts.

1. On the Start screen, type **user account**.

2. Tap or click User Accounts.

3. In the User Accounts dialog box, click or tap Change User Account Control Settings if you want to change when Windows 8.1 notifies you if programs are trying to make changes to your computer.

4. Tap or click Change Your Account Type if you want to change your account from Standard to Administrator or from Administrator to Standard.

5. To change the settings for another user account, click Manage Another Account.

6. In the Manage Accounts dialog box, click the user account you want to change.

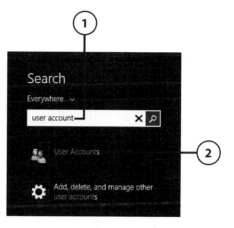

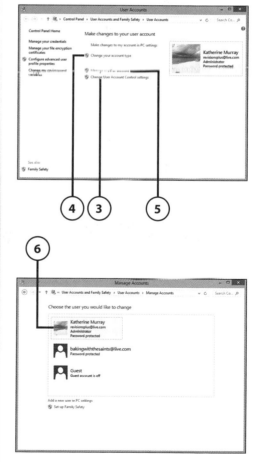

7. The Change an Account dialog box appears, listing options for the ways you can modify the selected account. You can add parental controls to the user account, change the account type (from Standard to Administrator or vice versa), or delete the account.

Add parental controls

Give user admin or standard privileges

WHO'S IN CHARGE HERE?

When you change the account type of a user's account from Standard to Administrator, you are giving that user permission to change settings on the computer, to create and delete user accounts, and to have access to all files and programs. If you want to limit the permissions another user has on your computer, assign the Standard account type, which allows the user to access programs and files but limits the person's ability to make changes that could affect the computing experience of other users.

Switching Users

You can easily switch among the user accounts on your Windows 8.1 computer by clicking or tapping your profile in the upper-right corner of the Windows 8.1 Start screen. You can sign out of Windows 8.1, lock your computer, or change users.

1. On the Start screen, click or tap the profile area (either your user-name or picture) in the upper-right corner of the screen. A menu opens.

2. Tap or click Lock to display your Lock screen and safeguard your computer. You might choose this when leaving your computer unattended for a while.

3. Tap or click Sign Out when you want to sign out of Windows 8.1, perhaps so that another user can log in.

4. Tap or click another user account to display the login screen for that account. The other user can enter the account password and click Submit to log in.

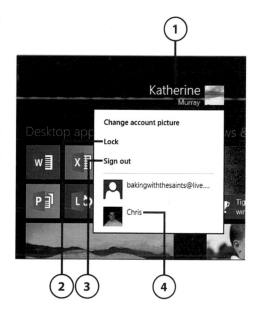

On Logging Out

If you log out of Windows 8.1, the next time you remove the Lock screen by swiping the touch-screen or pressing any key, all user accounts on your computer appear on the next screen so that you can tap or click the one you want to use to log in. You can then enter the password that goes along with that account to display the Windows 8.1 desktop.

Maintaining Your Privacy

One of the great things about Windows 8.1 is the easy way everything works together. You can easily share photos and files among apps, working with them online or off. Your apps can use your location data to set your time zone, display the weather, offer location-related search results, and much more.

On the flip side of all this sharing are two important questions: How do these apps share this information, and how much data do you really want to turn loose out there in cyberspace? Windows 8.1 lets you determine whether you want your apps to communicate with each other and share information about you—such as your location or content URLs from the apps you use— with others who are interested in gathering it.

Setting Location Privacy

To change your location privacy settings, follow these steps:

1. Display the PC Settings screen. (Tap or click the Settings charm and select Change PC Settings.) Tap or click Privacy in the list on the left side of the PC Settings window.

2. To keep your name, picture, and account Info private, slide the first setting to the Off position.

3. To have the SmartScreen Filter check content the Windows Store apps use, leave the second slider to the On position.

4. To turn off AutoText suggestions based on what you type and write, slide the third slider to Off.

5. If you want to disable the location sharing that goes on among your apps, slide the bottom slider to the Off position.

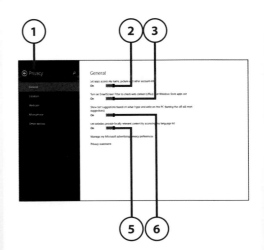

>>>Go Further

WHAT'S IN A PRIVACY STATEMENT?

When you click the Privacy Statement link on the Privacy screen, you are taken online to the Windows page where the statement is posted. This statement explains what personal information is gathered, what your choices are about it, and how the information is used.

All Apps view shows you
all your installed Windows
8.1 in one handy view.

The newly redesigned Windows
Store makes it easy for you to find
apps you can download and install.

This chapter shows you how to discover, start, and tweak apps in Windows 8.1 by teaching these tasks:

→ Getting started with apps

→ Finding and starting apps

→ Working with apps

→ Closing apps

→ Getting new apps from the Windows Store

→ Starting and stopping a program from the desktop

→ Repairing and uninstalling apps

Diving In with Apps

The vision of Windows 8.1 is an always-on, always-connected computing experience that is consistent no matter which Windows 8 computer or device you might be using. Microsoft hopes you will enjoy the various apps installed in Windows 8.1 for you and that you'll use them whether you're tapping and clicking your desktop PC, smartphone, or tablet.

The apps on the Windows 8.1 Start screen are colorful, and as you've no doubt already discovered, they provide helpful information that gives you updates at a glance. You might see the number of new email messages you've received, for example, or see what the temperature is outside, or catch a glimpse of the latest headlines in your favorite news app.

This chapter introduces you to the apps in Windows 8.1 and shows you how to find, launch, and work with them on your screen. You'll also learn how to find more apps in the Windows Store and download and install them easily in Windows 8.1.

Getting Started with Apps

Chapter 5, "Making It Your Windows 8.1," showed you how to change the color scheme and move app tiles around on the Start screen. You also learned how to create app groups so you could organize your apps in the way that makes the most sense to you. Windows 8.1 includes a number of apps you can use as soon as you fire up the operating system. You'll find what you need to check and send email, set appointments on your calendar, connect with others through instant messaging, catch up on the latest in your favorite social media accounts, and open Internet Explorer for some mindless browsing. These apps give you a good start on the types of tasks you'll want to accomplish in Windows 8.1, but this is only the beginning. You can download hundreds of apps from the Windows Store, and developers are posting new apps there all the time.

Some of the app tiles you see are *live tiles*, which continually update, showing information like the number of email messages you have to read, the current temperature in your city, the upcoming appointments on your calendar, or the headlines of your favorite news site. You learned how to change the way live tiles update—and turn off notifications entirely if you like—in Chapter 5.

Checking Out Your Apps

Early feedback for the first release of Windows 8 showed Microsoft that users really enjoy being able to see all their apps in a single view. So for Windows 8.1, Microsoft made it easier than ever to display all apps.

1. Swipe up from the bottom of the screen.

2. Or click the down arrow. The All Apps view appears.

3. Swipe or scroll to the left to display the full list of apps installed on your computer.

Pinning Apps to the Start Menu

As you look through all the apps on the Apps screen, you might discover a few you'd like to add to your Start screen. You can pin new apps easily—and unpin apps you no longer need—by following these steps:

1. Begin by displaying All Apps on your Windows 8 screen.

2. Swipe down on the app you want to select. Or, if you're using the mouse, right-click the app. The app options appear along the bottom of the screen.

3. Tap or click Pin to Start. The app you selected is added to the far-right end of the app tiles on your Start screen.

Moving Apps Around

You can easily move an app to any point on your Start screen by tapping and holding, or clicking, and dragging it to a new location. The other apps in the destination area move to make room for the new app. You can also arrange apps in groups and even name the groups so you can easily find the apps you're looking for. For more information on moving and grouping app tiles, refer to Chapter 5.

>>>Go Further

PIN TO TASKBAR?

You also might want to pin a particular app to the taskbar along the bottom of your Windows 8.1 desktop. This lets you easily launch an app from the Desktop without returning from the Start screen.

The app you pin to the taskbar appears in the Quick Launch area, toward the left end of the taskbar at the bottom of the screen. To learn more about using the desktop, refer to Chapter 4, "Working with the Desktop."

WHICH APPS ARE INCLUDED WITH WINDOWS 8.1?

🕐	Alarms	📧	Outlook.com
💗	Bing apps, including Health & Fitness, Food & Drink, News, Weather, Travel, Finance, Sports	👥	People
🧮	Calculator	🖼	Photos
📅	Calendar	📖	Reader
📷	Camera	☰	Reading List
🎮	Games	📐	Scan
🌐	Internet Explorer 11	☁	SkyDrive
✉	Mail	Ⓢ	Skype
🗺	Maps	🎤	Sound Recorder
🎧	Music	🎥	Video

Finding and Starting Apps

When you have dozens—or even hundreds—of apps in Windows 8.1, finding the specific one you want can be difficult. Anticipating that, Microsoft added a new Find in Start tool in the apps bar so you can easily locate the app you want. What's more, you can use Windows 8.1's powerful search tool to locate quickly just the app you're looking for.

Finding an App

You'll see the Find in Start tool on the apps bar in Windows 8.1 only when you've installed an app and it appears somewhere—but where?—on your Start screen. Here's how to use Find in Start to locate the app you need.

1. Display All Apps view by swiping up on the screen or clicking the down arrow.

2. Swipe down on or right-click the app tile for the app you want to find.

3. Click or tap Find in Start at the bottom of the screen. Windows 8.1 takes you to the Start screen, and the app you selected is high-lighted.

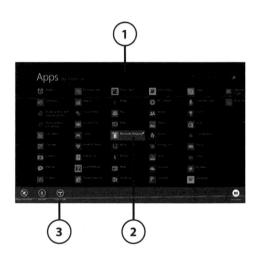

Locating an App

If the app you're looking for is already on your system, Windows 8.1 can also find it using search. You can simply type a few characters of the app's name and you'll be ready to go.

1. With the Start screen displayed, type the first few characters of the name of the app you're looking for. The search results screen appears immediately. If you're using a touch device, swipe in from the right to display the Charms bar and then tap in the search box. Your touch keyboard will appear, and you can type the first characters of the app's name.

2. Click or tap to choose where you want to search (Everywhere, Settings, Files, Web Images, or Web Videos).

3. Tap or click the result you want when it appears in the results list.

Downloading and Installing, Too

You'll learn more about what to do with the apps after you've found them, if they aren't already installed on your computer or device, later in this chapter.

Launching an App from the Start Screen

The easiest way to start a program on your Windows 8.1 computer is to simply scroll to the app you want on the Start screen and tap or click the app's tile.

1. Swipe or scroll through the apps on the Start screen.

2. Tap or click the tile of the app you want to start.

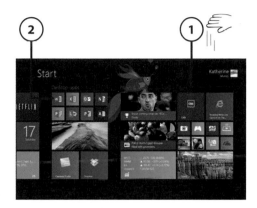

Launching an App on the Desktop

Some apps you add to Windows 8.1 will launch from the Start screen but will open on your desktop. This is the case when you use a legacy program—meaning a program that was available before the advent of Windows 8—and it requests permission to install a shortcut on your desktop. You can also add your favorite apps to the Windows desktop taskbar and create shortcuts for the desktop itself. (For more about making apps available on the desktop, refer to Chapter 4.)

1. On the Start screen, display your Windows desktop by scrolling to the Desktop tile and tapping or clicking it.

2. Locate the icon of the program you want to start, and double-tap or double-click it. The app launches and appears on your screen.

Adding Programs at Startup

If you have certain programs you want to launch as soon as your computer starts, you can add them to your Windows Startup folder. Even though the Windows 8.1 Start screen is a different animal from the Windows 8.1 desktop, you can still add apps you use regularly to your Startup folder using File Explorer. You might need to experiment a bit to see which apps work and which don't. Dropbox, for example, loaded fine during startup, but Windows Paint (my old friend) gave me an error. To add an app to your Startup folder, use File Explorer (available on your Windows desktop) to locate the program file. Then copy and paste it in your Startup folder. The next time you log in to Windows 8 and display the desktop, your program will open automatically.

Quick Launch bar

System notification tray

Working with Apps

You might have noticed that there really aren't many *windows* in Windows 8.1 anymore. When you launch an app from the Start screen, it zooms to take up your full screen (even though you can tile the display to show more than one app, as you'll learn in this section).

When you launch an app that runs on the Desktop, you might see a more traditional window with the familiar Minimize and Close buttons in the upper-right corner. This section shows you the differences between traditional apps and newer apps in Windows 8.1 so you know how to find your way around each type.

Switching Among Open Programs

Similar to the way you moved from one program to another in previous versions of Windows, you can still cycle through open apps by pressing Alt+Tab in Windows 8.1. A small message box appears in the center of the desktop area showing you all your currently open programs. Each time you press Tab while holding Alt, Windows 8.1 moves to the next open program available on your computer. Release the keys when the app you want to use is highlighted

Exploring a Program "Window"

Depending on the type of app you open, it might appear in the Windows 8.1 style or in the more traditional desktop style. If the app you launch hasn't yet been designed for Windows 8.1, you will see a more traditional window with a title bar, scrollbars, and the like. If the app has been designed for Windows 8.1, the app will open in a windowless frame and fill your screen.

Title bar   **Ribbon**   **Windows controls**

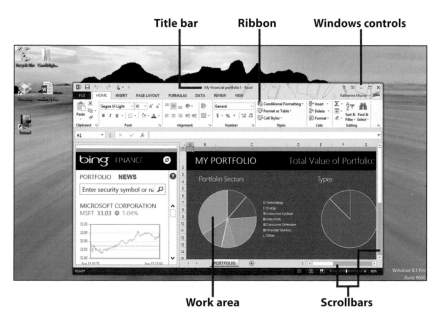

Work area   **Scrollbars**

- **Title bar**—The title bar of the window shows you the name of the file you're working on and the name of the application program in which it was created.

- **Window controls**—In the upper-right corner of the program window, you can find three tools to change the state of the window. Minimize reduces the window to the taskbar; Restore Down reduces the window to its previous smaller size (or, if the window is already at a smaller size, it changes to Maximize, which makes the window full size); and Close, which closes the file and, if no other files are open for that program, closes the program as well.

- **Ribbon or menu bar**—The Ribbon is a feature common to some legacy programs, offering the tools and options you need for working with various programs. You instead might see a menu bar listing menu names close to the top of the window. You can click a menu name to display a list of tools you can use in your program.

- **Scrollbars**—Depending on the size of your file and the type of program you are using, you might see horizontal and vertical scrollbars.

- **Work area**—The work area of the window is the place where you write documents, create worksheets, edit photos, and more. The file you open and work with appears in the work area.

Checking Out a Windows 8.1 App

Windows 8.1 apps are designed to look and act much different from a traditional app. When you tap or click a tile to launch an app that has been designed for Windows 8.1, the app will launch full-screen and you will navigate the program without the menu bars, Windows controls, and tools you might be accustomed to in legacy programs.

Hopefully, even though the experience is much different from traditional programs, you will find it easy to understand. If you've been using a touch device—such as a smartphone or tablet—the gestures you use to interact with the operating system might already be second nature to you.

App appears full screen

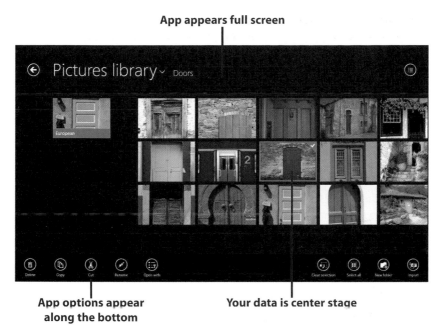

App options appear along the bottom

Your data is center stage

- **Full screen**—As soon as you tap an app tile to launch the program, it opens full-screen on your display.

- **Your data, center-stage**—The content of the app is really the main focus on the screen.

- **App options within reach**—You can easily swipe up from the bottom of the app to display the options available to you as you work with your information.

Moving Among Open Apps

You can have many apps open at one time in Windows 8.1. But how do you know which ones are open when they're out of sight? And how do you choose the one you want to appear next? Windows 8.1 includes a feature known as the "apps panel" that shows small thumbnails of your open apps in a panel along the left side of the screen. The apps panel enables you to see the apps you have open in Windows 8.1. Now you can "bump" your mouse against the upper-left corner of the screen and drag downward to display the apps panel. You can then click or tap the app you want to move to or drag it to the center of the screen.

1. Move the mouse to the upper-left corner of the screen and "bump" the mouse against the edge. The top thumbnail appears.

2. Move the mouse downward along the left edge. Additional thumbnails appear.

3. Click the thumbnail of the app you want to display, or drag it to the center of the screen.

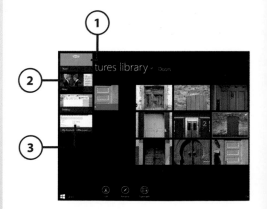

>>>Go Further

CYCLING THROUGH APPS

In the initial release of Windows 8, you could drag apps in from the left by touching along the left edge and dragging your finger to the right. Windows 8.1 still has this option, but now that action isn't the default. In Windows 8.1, when you drag in from the left, the apps panel appears. You can then tap the app you want to use and drag it to the center of the screen to make it front and center.

To change the default so you can cycle through apps by dragging them in from the left, tap or click the Settings charm, select Change PC Settings, and tap or click PC & Devices. Next, tap Corners & Edges. Then, in the App Switching settings, slide to the On position the setting When I Swipe In from the Left Edge, Switch between My Recent Apps Instead of Showing a List of Them. (This whole process takes about three clicks, so it's easier than it sounds.)

Tiling and snapping apps with Windows 8 proper, it was a pretty big deal to be able to arrange two apps open on the screen at once. You could pull in an app from the left and then snap it up toward the top of the screen to anchor it in place. Now in Windows 8.1, the snap functionality is greatly improved and supports you having as many as four apps open on the screen at once, if you have the screen resolution to support that.

For example, you might want to have OneNote open along with email while you browse using Internet Explorer 11. Or perhaps you want to watch a movie while you play a game. Whatever apps you want to run at the same time, you'll tile them and place them side-by-side to do it. You can also still cycle through other apps, even while two are tiled. Nice.

1.   Open the apps you want to use.

2.   To anchor an app, drag it in from the left to the right side of the screen and flick it toward the top of your screen.

Get Me Back to Full-Screen

When you want to do away with the tiling effect, tap or click the divider and drag it to the right, off the right edge of the screen. The app that was in the left window then becomes the only app visible on your screen.

Closing Apps

One of the surprising things about the earliest versions of Windows 8 was that you didn't need to close any app you had opened. Apps that aren't the current focus immediately go into suspended mode; this is one of the ways Windows 8 saves power. But not having a way to close programs just seemed odd to those of us who have been trained over the years to finish what we start, put away our toys (thanks, Mom), and exit correctly from any program we are using.

In response to public feedback, developers added a close procedure to Windows 8. Now you can swipe down to put an app away, effectively removing it from memory—which, of course, it already did itself when it went into suspended mode. But now we can feel better about it.

Closing Selected Apps

When you're ready to put away an app you've been working with, closing it is a simple matter. First, save any file you were working with, and then follow these steps:

1. Touch at the top of the screen and swipe down or, if you're using a mouse, position the mouse pointer at the top of the screen. Then press and hold the mouse while dragging down toward the bottom edge of the screen.

2. The app reduces to a small window, and as you swipe it downward, it disappears completely.

Using the Task Manager

You can also close open apps by using the Task Manager. The Task Manager has been significantly revamped in Windows 8.1 to give you all kinds of information about how much processing power each app is using. Of course, for some of us, this type of information is overkill, so by default Windows 8.1 gives you the simple version of Task Manager to work with.

1. Press Ctrl+Alt+Delete and click Task Manager to display the Task Manager window. Or, if you're on a touch device, swipe in from the right to display the Charms bar and tap Search. Tap in the search box and your touch keyboard appears. Type **Task Manager** and the utility appears in the result list. Tap Task Manager to open it.

2. To close a specific app, tap or click the one you want to close.

3. If you want to see how much processing power each app is using, tap or click More Details.

4. Review the amount of processing power, memory, disk space, and network access each app is currently using.

5. You can also view detailed information about each app by tapping or clicking the various tabs at the top of the detailed Task Manager display.

6. To return to the simple display, tap or click Fewer Details.

7. Tap or click End Task if you want to close the selected app.

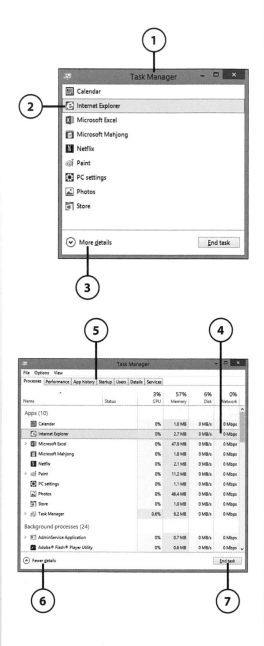

>>>Go Further

ASSESSING WHAT YOU WANT AT STARTUP

One great feature the detailed version of Task Manager offers is an evaluation of how much impact the apps you load automatically at startup are having on your computer's performance.

Display the Task Manager by pressing Ctrl+Alt+Delete or, on your tablet, by searching for Task Manager and tapping the utility when it appears. In the Task Manager, select More Details to see the full set of data available to you in relation to the current apps. Tap or click the Startup tab at the top of the Task Manager dialog box. In the Startup Impact column, on the far-right side of the dialog box, you see how Windows 8.1 rates the impact the various apps have on the startup routine. If you see an app that is rated as having a High impact, you can select it and then tap or click Disable to keep it from loading automatically. You might find that Windows 8.1 boots faster after you've disabled high-impact apps.

Getting Apps from the Revamped Windows Store

When Windows 8 initially launched, folks were glad to have an app store to browse for new apps, but they weren't thrilled with the way the Store was executed. Apps weren't easy to find and lacked the detailed descriptions most people were looking for.

In Windows 8.1, the Windows Store has been completely redesigned. Now there is a more open look and feel, with detailed information about apps that are relevant to the types of things you like to do. The whole experience is more dynamic, is powered by Bing, and presents apps targeted to users' interests.

Another big change in the Windows Store is that when you're purchasing an app, you get to use real money instead of Microsoft Points. You can also purchase gift cards and add money to your accounts, just the way you did using Microsoft Points.

Introducing the Windows Store

The Windows Store app tile appears in the easy-to-find location at the far-left end of your Windows 8.1 Start screen. The Store app tile has a live tile notification telling you the number of apps you currently have installed that now have updates available through the Windows Store.

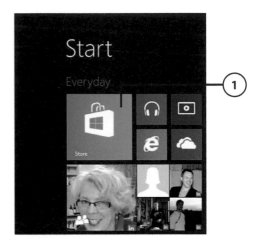

1. Launch the Windows Store by tapping or clicking the Store app tile.

2. Scroll by swiping or using the mouse to look through apps off the right side of the screen. As you scroll to the right, you'll see the following categories: Picks for You, Popular Now, New Releases, Top Paid, and Top Free.

3. Tap the tile of the app you want to download.

Swipe down to display Store options

Search for apps

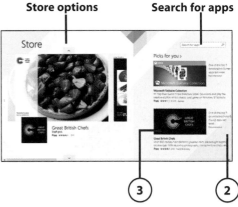

Searching for an App

Now with the Windows Store you can search within the app for the specific app or apps you want to find. You can also use Search within Windows 8.1 if you like, but you'll get a mix of results from all software locations. To search only within the Windows Store, open the app and use the search tool that appears in the upper-right corner.

1. Display the Windows Store.

2. Tap or click in the search tool and type a word or phrase you want to search for. A listing of possible apps appears.

3. Tap or click an app in the short list if you see the one you want.

4. Tap or click the Search tool to do a full search. Windows 8.1 displays a search results page with the first items that meet your criteria.

5. Click to choose a different category if you like.

6. Select the price of the app you're looking for.

7. Click to sort the apps by relevance, displaying the newest apps first, the ones with the highest rating, or the ones with the lowest price, for example.

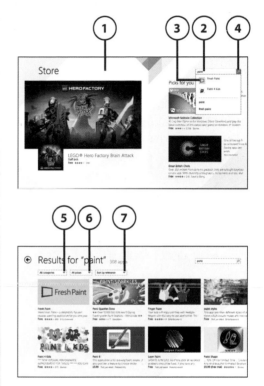

Categories in the Windows Store

When you're searching for apps in the Windows Store, you can narrow down your search if you don't know a specific name by clicking or tapping the category arrow and choosing the category you want from the list that appears: Games, Social, Entertainment, Photo, Music & Video, Sports, Books & Reference, News & Weather, Health & Fitness, Food & Dining, Lifestyle, Shopping, Travel, Finance, Productivity, Tools, Security, Business, Education, Government, and Update Windows.

Installing an App

After you find the app you want, you can click or tap the app tile and the app opens on the screen. You'll find out more about the app, see how users have rated it (and how many users have weighed in), and learn more about the app's specific features. The information page also shows you pictures of the app in action. If you decide this app is worth a closer look, you can install the app and the Windows Store will download and install it on your computer or device.

1. Scroll through the app information and determine whether you want to install the app.

2. Tap or click Install. Windows 8.1 displays a small "Installing" notification in the upper-right corner of your screen; when the installation is complete, a notification lets you know.

   You can view the new app when you display All Apps view. You can add the new app to the Start screen if you like by swiping down on the tile (or right-clicking it) and tapping or clicking Pin to Start. You can move the app to any group you like by tapping or clicking and dragging the app to that group. Then, just tap or click the app tile to launch your new app.

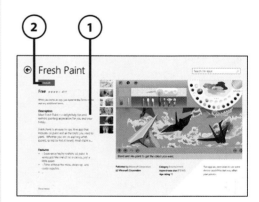

Managing Your Apps

Windows 8.1 lets you easily see which apps you've installed and manage the financial aspect of your Microsoft account while you're in the Windows Store.

1. Display the Windows Store.

2. Swipe down or right-click at the top of the screen. A Windows Store panel appears, showing three buttons—Home, Your Apps, and Your Account—at the top of the categories panel.

3. Click or tap Your Apps to see a list of all the apps currently installed on your computer.

4. Tap or click Your Account to review your Microsoft account address along with the credit card you've set up to go along with that account.

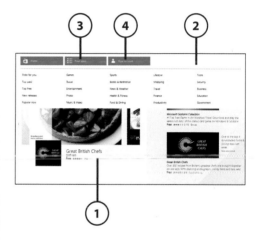

Starting and Stopping an App from the Desktop

As you learned in Chapter 4, many of the apps you open on the Start screen can actually run on the Windows 8.1 Desktop, depending on whether they have been released in the new Windows 8.1 style. For example, when you open one of the Office 2013 apps, it launches from the Start screen but opens on the Windows desktop, and you have the traditional window border and Ribbon, complete with its tools, available for your use.

To make launching apps easier (if you're working on the Desktop anyway), you can add shortcuts to the desktop taskbar (you learn how to do that in Chapter 4). This section shows you how to start and close an app from the Windows 8.1 Desktop.

Starting a Program from the Desktop

If you've added shortcuts to your Windows desktop or pinned an app to the taskbar so you could launch it easily while you're working there, you have only one very simple step to take to launch the program. Start by displaying the Desktop; just tap or click the Desktop app tile on your Windows 8.1 Start screen.

1. Double-click, or double-tap, the program icon.

2. The program opens on the desktop, and you can work with it as you normally would.

Be My BFF Program

If you want to add a favorite desktop program to the Start screen so you can launch it easily from there without searching for it, try this: Right-click the pro-gram icon on the Desktop and tap or click Pin to Start. This adds the icon to the far-right side of the apps list on the Start screen (although you can drag the app tile anywhere you want it to appear). Now you'll be able to launch the program from the Start screen, but it will still open on the desktop.

Do More Before You Jump

As you learned in Chapter 4, jump lists give you an easy way to start a program and open a file at the same time, but you can perform other file actions as well. Right-click the file in the jump list to display a context menu that enables you to open, print, copy, or display the file properties. You can also pin the file to the list or remove it from the list altogether.

Exiting the Program

When you're ready to close the program you've been working with on the desktop, shutting it down is a simple matter. First, save any file you were working with, and then follow these steps:

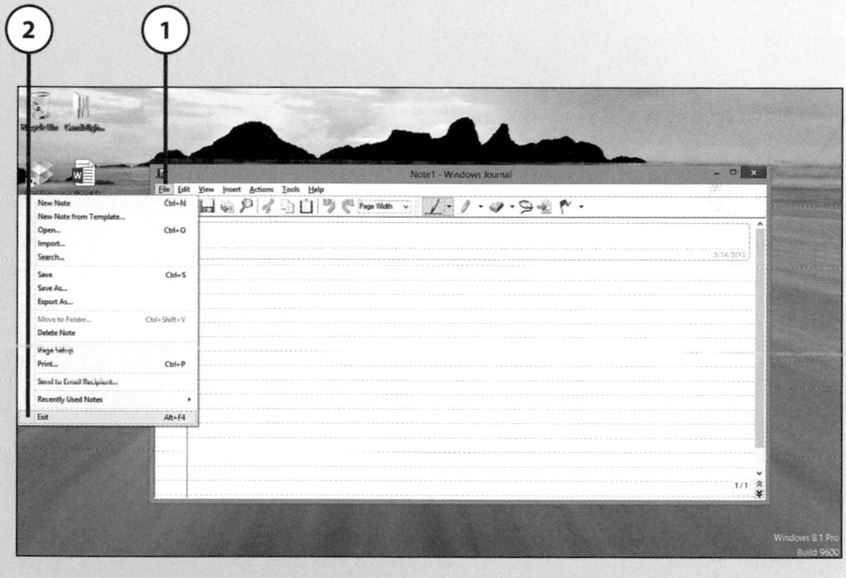

1. Click the File tab or, if the program is a non-Microsoft program, click the File menu. This is typically the menu farthest left on the menu bar.

2. Click Exit. Some programs might ask you to confirm that you do in fact want to close the program. If you see a prompt, click Yes to finish exiting the program.

Quicker Closing

You can also exit a program by clicking the X button at the upper-right corner of any open window.

Repairing and Uninstalling Programs

Windows 8.1 has a tool you can use—which is actually a holdover from Windows 7—that enables you to safely repair and uninstall programs. You can find what you need in the Programs category of the Control Panel.

Repairing Installations

If you have a program that begins misbehaving by locking up when you open a certain template, taking forever to check for your email, or giving you errors when you try to choose a specific tool, Windows might be able to repair the installation for you. Not all programs offer Change or Repair options, but for the ones that do, you can use the tools in the Programs category of the Control Panel to correct any errors that are making your programs behave inconsistently.

1. On the Start screen, start typing **control panel**, and the Search tool appears immediately and results are shown in the Apps side of the screen.

2. Tap or click Control Panel.

3. Tap or click Programs.

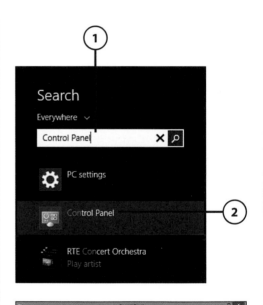

4. Tap or click Programs and Features.

5. In the program listing, click the name of the program you want to repair.

6. Click Repair. Windows launches the install utility to correct the problem. Choose the repair option you want Windows to use.

7. When the repair operation finishes, click the Close button to exit Control Panel.

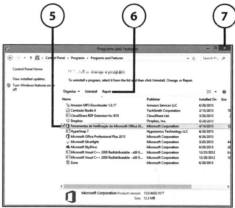

AND DON'T FORGET TO REFRESH ONCE IN A WHILE

>>>Go Further

You can refresh your computer—using the Refresh tool—if you begin having problems like slow processing speeds or quirky program behaviors. Refreshing your PC wipes away settings and configurations that could be causing problems, but it won't do anything to your programs or data. You can run Refresh by tapping the Settings charm, selecting Change PC Settings, tapping or clicking Update & Recovery, and then tapping or clicking Recovery. In the Refresh Your PC Without Affecting Your Files area, tap Get Started to begin the refresh process.

You learned about this refreshing process in Chapter 2, "Preparing Your PC and Setting Up Devices."

Uninstalling Programs

You can also remove programs you no longer need to free up space on your hard drive and allow room for other programs. When you know you don't need one of your programs anymore, you can uninstall it easily.

1. On the Start screen, type **uninstall**. Search results appear.

2. Tap Uninstall a Program. The Program and Features dialog box appears, listing the programs you have installed. Notice that your apps do not appear in this list. (You'll learn how to uninstall apps in the next section.)

3. Tap or click the name of the program you want to uninstall.

4. Tap or click Uninstall. Windows launches a wizard that will remove the program from your computer.

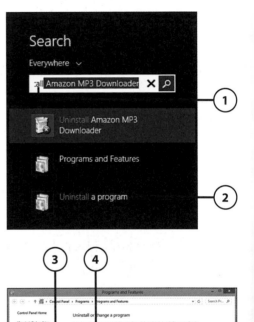

Uninstalling Apps

In Chapter 3, "Using and Tweaking the Start Screen," you learned how to remove an app from the Windows 8.1 Start screen to free up room for other apps. The process for uninstalling an app you no longer want in Windows 8.1 is a similar process. Here's how to do it:

1. On the Start screen, select the app you want to uninstall by swiping down on the app tile or right-clicking it.

2. The apps bar appears along the bottom of the Start screen. To uninstall the app, tap or click Uninstall.

3. Windows 8.1 lets you know what you're removing. Tap or click Uninstall to complete the process.

This PC shows you your primary folders as well as devices and drives and network locations available to your PC.

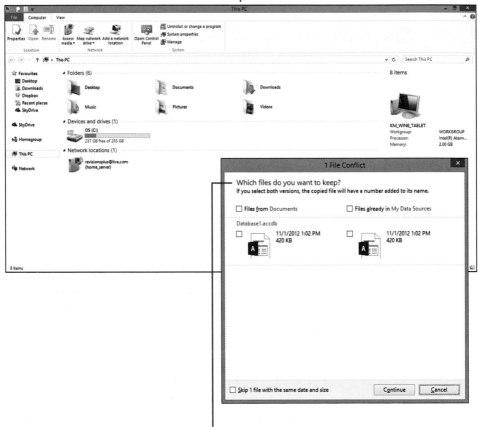

File Explorer helps you resolve file conflicts during copy operations.

This chapter shows you how to use File Explorer to organize your folders and files by exploring these tasks:

→ Getting started with File Explorer
→ Using the ribbon
→ Managing your files and folders
→ Copying, moving, and sharing files and folders

Organizing Files with File Explorer

File Explorer is the name of the Windows 8.1 tool you'll use to find, copy, paste, move, and organize your files and folders—both on your computer and in the cloud. You launch File Explorer by clicking or tapping a tile on the desktop. If you've previously used Windows Explorer (in Windows 7, for example), you'll quickly find your way around.

The big change File Explorer offers in Windows 8.1 is actually a disappearance. Gone are the libraries that used to appear in the left navigation panel by default. My Documents, My Pictures, and My Music are now hidden when you launch File Explorer for the first time and the contents and devices of your PC—appropriately named *This PC*—appear instead. If you are a fan of libraries, however, don't despair; you can still add your own libraries and display the ones that make your life easier.

This chapter shows you the basics of working with File Explorer so you can organize your folders and files in the way that makes the most sense to you. And that, of course, makes the ho-hum tasks faster so you can get on to the things you'd *rather* be doing on your Windows 8.1 PC.

Getting Started with File Explorer

You launch File Explorer from the Windows 8.1 Desktop, which means you must tap or click the Desktop tile on the Start screen before you can get to the point where you can start File Explorer. On the Desktop, you'll find File Explorer in the Quick Launch bar in the lower-left corner of your screen.

Add File Explorer to the Start Screen

Swipe up from the bottom of the Start screen or click the down arrow at the bottom of the screen. All apps view is displayed. Scroll to the far-right end of the apps list, and in the Windows System group of apps, swipe down on or right-click the File Explorer icon. In the apps bar, tap or click Pin to Start. Now File Explorer will appear as a tile on your Start screen, and you can launch the tool without displaying your Desktop. To find out more about how to pin an app to the Start screen, see Chapter 7, "Diving In with Apps."

Starting File Explorer

The easiest way to launch File Explorer is to click or tap the icon that looks like a folder in the Quick Launch bar on the left side of the taskbar on the Windows 8.1 desktop. File Explorer opens in a window on your screen. The first time you start File Explorer, the ribbon is hidden. Display it by clicking Expand the Ribbon in the upper-right corner of File Explorer.

Click or tap the File Explorer icon.

Touring the File Explorer Screen

Although the ribbon adds some aesthetic and functional value to File Explorer, much of what the program offers was available in Windows 7 as well. Here are the key elements on the File Explorer screen you'll be working with:

- **Location bar**—The Location bar shows the currently displayed folder.

- **Refresh button**—The Refresh button updates the display to show the files in the current folder.

- **Search box**—You can use the search box to find folders and files in File Explorer.

- **Navigation pane**—The Navigation pane displays your favorites, folders, and files on your computer.

- **This PC**—This PC displays by default the primary folders on your computer and any devices and networks to which your system is connected.

- **Minimize the ribbon**—Use this tool to both hide and display the File Explorer ribbon.

- **Get Help**—Click Get Help to display a pop-up window of help information related to the task you were performing in File Explorer.

Switching Between the Preview and Details Pane

You'll use the panel on the left side of File Explorer to get more information about a file you're working with. File Explorer includes two views—the Preview pane and the Details pane—that act as a toggle. When you click or tap the View tab and display the Preview pane, you see a preview of the contents of the file. When you tap or click Details pane, the Preview pane is replaced by a pane that shows you when the file was last modified, the size of the file, whether the file is shared, and other file details.

Checking Out This PC

When you start File Explorer, the tool opens with This PC selected in the navigation pane. Your This PC view offers you top-level access to your content, organized by type or location. By default, these folders are displayed in This PC: Desktop, Documents, Downloads, Music, Pictures, and Video. You also might see folders related to any networks you use and one that gives you access to Windows files. You'll also be able to see at a glance which devices and drives are connected to your PC. And finally, the This PC view displays any network locations you have access to while you're using that computer.

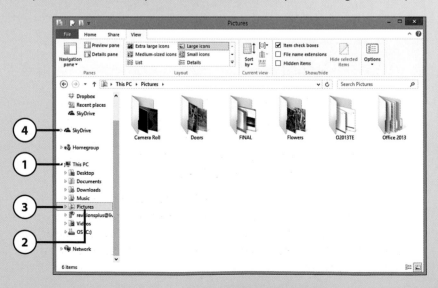

1. Click or tap This PC in the navigation pane. The list of primary folders appears beneath your selection.

2. Select the folder with the files you want to view.

3. Click the arrow to display subfolders.

4. Select SkyDrive to see files stored in the online storage connected to your Microsoft account.

Where Did the Libraries Go?

Windows 8.1 changes the way libraries appear. In fact, at first, they don't appear at all. You'll notice some overlap of features between This PC and libraries you might have used in previous versions of Windows or File Explorer. To display libraries, click the Navigation Pane tool in the View tab and select Show Libraries.

Changing the File Explorer Layout

You can hide and redisplay the various panes in File Explorer: Details, Preview, and Navigation. Tap or click the View tab and in the Panes group on the left of the ribbon, select the pane you want to display. If you deselect both the Preview pane and the Details pane, the center pane will extend to show only the files and subfolders in the currently selected folder. You can also tap or click the Navigation pane arrow to display a menu of options for changing the way the Navigation pane displays folders and favorites. To redisplay a pane you've hidden, tap or click the pane to select the one you want to show.

Using the Ribbon

The File Explorer ribbon offers the tools you need based on what you're trying to do. Even the major tabs change, depending on what you've selected. If you choose This PC, for example, the tabs that appear are File, Computer, and View. But if you select one of the folders in the This PC group, the tabs will be File, Home, Share, and View.

In addition to the primary tabs, the File Explorer tab displays contextual tabs that appear only when you've selected a specific something. For example, when you click one or more picture files, the Picture Tools contextual tab appears above the ribbon. When you click outside the picture file, the Picture Tools tab disappears.

Learning the Ribbon Layout

The tabs in File Explorer group all the tools you need for working with your files and folders.

The File tab gives you access to the folders you use frequently. You can also work with the command prompt, delete the file history, display help, and close File Explorer.

File		
	Open **n**ew window ▸	**Frequent places**
		1 Articles
	Open command **p**rompt ▸	2 ch 06
		3 ch 07
	Open Windows Powe**r**Shell ▸	4 Figures
		5 ch 03
		6 ch 01
	Delete history ▸	7 ch 05
		8 ch 02
	Help ▸	9 ch 04
		Figures
	Close	

The Home tab provides common tools you'll use for copying and pasting files and paths; moving, deleting, and renaming files and folders; adding folders; opening files and folders; displaying file and folder properties; and selecting files and folders.

The Share tab contains tools for sharing the content you've selected, whether you want to email the files or folders, compress them into a ZIP file, share them with your HomeGroup, or fine-tune the security settings assigned to the file or folder.

The View tab includes tools you can use to change the way the File Explorer window appears. You can use the tools in the View tab to set up File Explorer the way you want it, displaying the Navigation pane, the Preview or Details pane, the size of the icons you want to use, and the data that will be either hidden or displayed. You can also add columns, sort files, and select from a number of layouts in the File Explorer screen.

Different Tabs in This PC

You might be flummoxed at first when you're looking for the tabs you need and see File, Computer, and View instead of the traditional tabs. These tabs appear when This PC is selected. Click the folder with the files you want to work with, and you'll see the tabs you expect: File, Home Share, and View.

Recognizing Contextual Tabs

You'll know when you're looking at a contextual tab on the File Explorer ribbon because it looks different from the regular tabs. The regular tabs are white and gray—the selected tab appears white, and the other tabs appear gray. But when you've selected a file, a folder, or another object in File Explorer, a contextual tab related to the item you selected appears in a light orange shade along the top of the ribbon. When you click the contextual tab, you'll find tools that enable you to work specifically with the file or folder you've selected.

Showing and Hiding the File Explorer Ribbon

When the ribbon was first introduced with Office 2007, some people weren't too crazy about it, in part because it dramatically changed the way we find the tools we need in our programs. The ribbon was tweaked in Office 2010 so it would be a bit more intuitive for folks to use. Some users feel the ribbon takes up too much room on the screen, so in subsequent versions of Office and in other Microsoft tools, such as File Explorer, Microsoft made the ribbon easy to hide, if that's your preference.

1. You can hide the ribbon by tapping the Minimize the Ribbon tool.

2. Display the ribbon by tapping or clicking the same tool, which is now called the Expand the Ribbon tool.

>>>Go Further

MORE TOOLS WITHIN REACH: THE QUICK ACCESS TOOLBAR

File Explorer also has a Quick Access toolbar in the upper-left corner of the Explorer window. The Quick Access toolbar gives you a small, customizable set of tools you can get to easily. It's always within easy clicking or tapping reach.

By default, the Quick Access toolbar in File Explorer shows only the Properties and New Folder tools, but you can tap or click the Customize Quick Access Toolbar arrow next to the New Folder tool to display options that enable you to add undo, redo, delete, and rename tools if you like. To add a tool, simply click or tap the one you want to add to the toolbar. To remove a tool, tap or click the arrow again and then tap or click a selected tool to remove the check mark. The tool is removed from the toolbar.

You can also choose a different position for the Quick Access toolbar by tapping or clicking the Customize arrow and selecting Show Below the Ribbon. This moves the Quick Access toolbar so that it appears beneath the ribbon but above the Location bar. There's also a command that suppresses the display of the ribbon in the Quick Access toolbar menu; to hide the ribbon, click or tap Minimize the Ribbon.

Get the Scoop on Your Tools

File Explorer now also has new hotkey tool tips that tell you the name of the tool, give you a short description, and (in some cases) display the shortcut key for using the tool. All you need to do is hover the mouse over an item you're wondering about.

LIBRARY CHANGES IN WINDOWS 8.1

>>Go Further

One of the big changes in Windows 8.1 is that you'll no longer find libraries in the navigation pane along the left side of the File Explorer screen. In previous versions of Windows, libraries are different from actual folders in which specific files are stored; instead, they are indexed locations of a specific type of files. The library gathers the files together so you can find them easily. When you click a library to view its contents, what you're really seeing are links to the files stored in their respective folders.

Libraries are being phased out in Windows 8.1 because the primary folders in This PC enable you to do basically the same tasks you performed with libraries (and you'll notice the overlap in the folder and library names). What's more, the enhanced search capabilities in Windows 8.1 make it easy for you to locate the files you need quickly and easily, and the easy access of cloud storage in the navigation pane further puts your files within reach.

Even though libraries are hidden in Windows 8.1, you can still display them and work with them by clicking the Navigation Pane tool in the View tab and selecting Show Libraries. You can also create new libraries of your own by right-clicking or tapping and holding the folder you want to use to create a new library; then select Include in Library and select Create New Library. Windows 8.1 displays the libraries and shows the new library you added.

Managing Your Files and Folders

A lot of what you do in File Explorer involves finding, organizing, and sharing your files. You will probably work with document files, picture files, music files, video files, and more. Knowing how to locate, select, copy, move, sort, and get information about your files is an important part of staying organized and up-to-speed with all the data you're collecting. Organizing your folders so they are where you can get to them easily will help you find what you need quickly so you can get back to work (or play).

Finding Files and Folders

Finding the files and folders you're looking for in File Explorer is super simple. You can enter a word or phrase in the Search box for a simple search, or refine your search by searching for a specific date, kind of file, size, or other file properties.

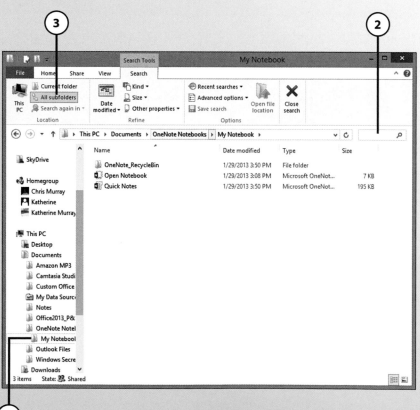

1. Begin by tapping or clicking the folder (for example, Documents, Music, Pictures, or Videos) or the drive where you want to search.

2. Tap or click in the search box, and type a word or phrase to describe what you're searching for. The Search Tools Search contextual tab appears above the ribbon.

3. In the Location group, tap or click whether you want to search your entire computer, search the current folder, or include all subfolders in your search.

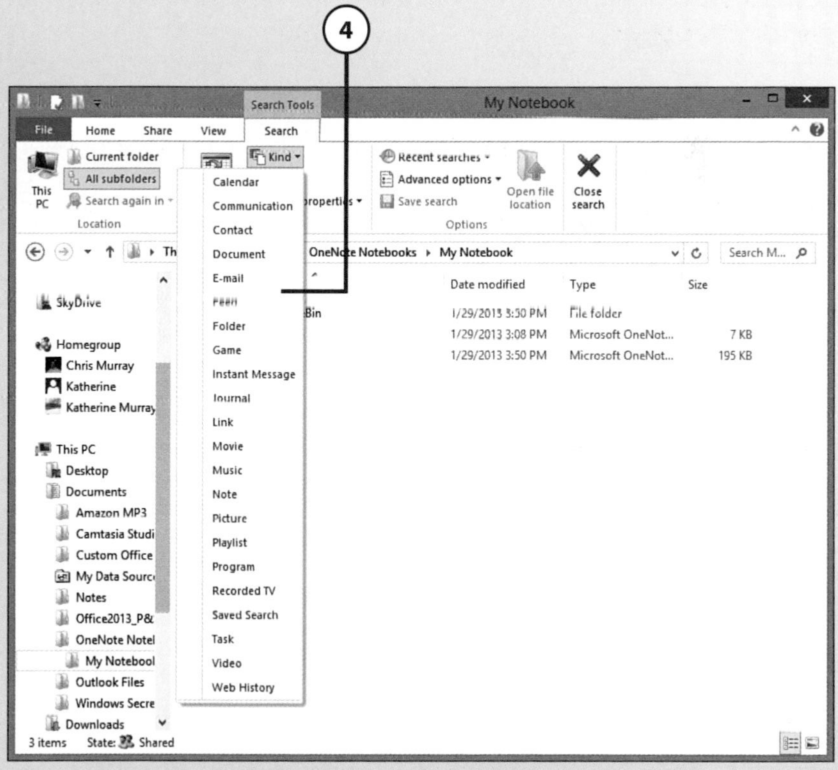

4. In the Refine group of the Search Tools Search tab, tap or click a search filter if you want to apply one: Date Modified, Kind, Size, or Other Properties.

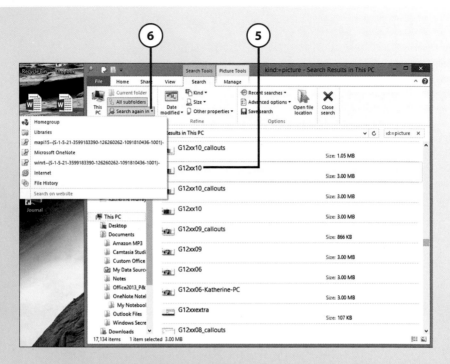

5. Tap or click the search result you want to see.

6. If you want to repeat the search in a different location, select Search Again in the Location group and click or tap your choice.

Finding Specific File Types

When you want to find files in a specific format—for example, .jpg, .wmv, .docx, or .mp3—use the Type filter in the Other Properties tool in the Refine group. When you click Type, File Explorer displays a list box of file formats you can choose to narrow your search, and you can tap or click the one that fits what you're searching for.

>>>Go Further

SAVING YOUR SEARCHES

If you find that you often perform the same searches—perhaps you search for the latest podcasts or look for the newest video clips that have been added to your computer—you can save the search so you can use it again later.

Enter the search information as usual, and then, when the search results appear in the File Explorer window, tap or click Save Search in the Options group of the Search Tools Search tab. The Save As dialog box appears. Type a filename for the saved search, and tap or click Save.

Now you can use the search at any time by tapping or clicking the saved search in the Favorites area at the top of the Navigation pane.

Selecting Files and Folders

The Home tab of File Explorer gives you the tools you need to select files and folders easily.

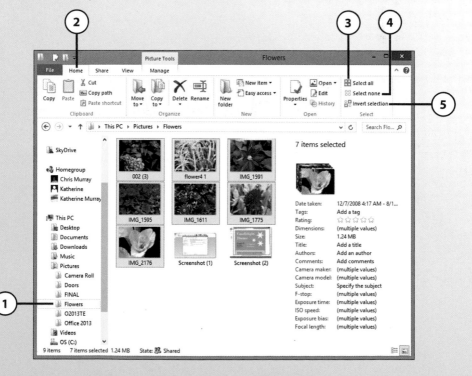

1. In the Navigation pane, click or tap the drive, library, or folder where you want to select files.

2. Click or tap the Home tab.

3. If you want to select all contents of the selected folder, tap or click Select All in the Select group.

4. If you want to deselect any files or folders you've previously selected, click or tap Select None.

5. If you have previously selected multiple files (by pressing Ctrl and clicking files or tapping multiple selections) and want to change the selection to all those that were previously unselected, tap or click Invert Selection.

Viewing File Information

You can change the way you view the files in the folders you select by using the tools in the View tab.

The Panes group on the far-left side of the ribbon contains tools you can use to preview the selected file or display details about the file you've chosen.

1. Click or tap the library or folder containing the file you want to see.

2. Use Search if necessary to locate the file.

3. Click or tap the View tab.

4. Tap or click Preview Pane in the Panes group if you want to see a preview of the file.

5. Tap or click Details Pane if you want to see the details of the file.

What Do You Mean, *Details*?

The Details pane of File Explorer gives you information about the selected file. You can see the filename, size, and date it was last modified. You can also see any tags that have been assigned to the file, review the authors' names, and (in some cases) see any rating that has been applied to the file.

Tagging Files

The information in the Details pane isn't just for viewing—you can also change the information and save it while you're there. By just clicking or tapping in the Tags area and typing the tags you want to add, you can categorize your files so you can find them more easily when you search for them later.

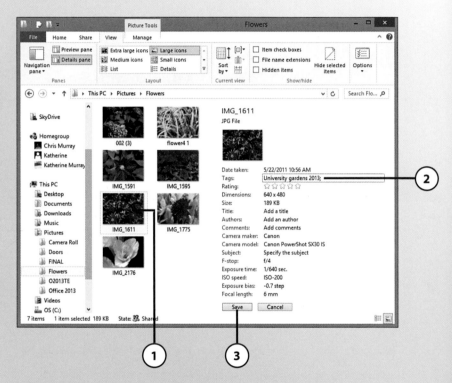

1. Select the file you want to tag in File Explorer.

2. In the Details pane, tap or click in the Tags field. Type tags you can use to identify or categorize the file, separating multiple tags with semicolons.

3. Click or tap Save.

Tagging Again Later

The next time you add tags, when you tap or click in the Tag field and start typing, File Explorer displays a list box, suggesting tags you've entered previously. Click or tap the check box of any tag you want to add, and click or tap Save to save the tags.

RATING FILES

In the Details pane of your picture files, you can also assign a rating value to your image files. Rating the files on your computer helps you prioritize the ones you love over the ones you don't. This can help you select the right files when you're searching, for example, for the best photos you have of a particular event. If you've rated the files, you can search for the files with the highest rating, which will give you a results list that is the cream of the crop. Select the file you want to rate in File Explorer, and then click or tap the number of stars (one to five) you want to assign to the image. Tap or click Save to save your rating.

Arranging Folder Display

Chances are your folders contain lots of files, and that means you need to think about the best way to display them so you can easily find what you need. File Explorer gives you the ability to filter your files so they are displayed in the order you prefer. You might choose to arrange the files by Author, Date Modified, Tag, Type, or Name, for example.

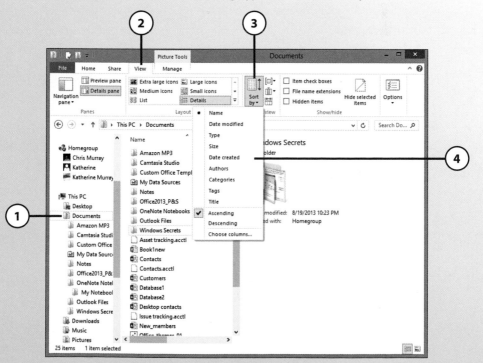

1. Click or tap the folder you want to arrange in the Navigation pane.

2. Click or tap the View tab.

3. Click or tap the Sort By option in the Current View group. A list of options appears.

4. Click the setting that arranges the files the way you want them to appear. Authors lists the files and folders alphabetically by author; Date Modified lists files with the most recently modified files shown first; Tags arranges files alphabetically according to any tags you've assigned to the file; Type shows the files organized by file type; and Name lists the files alphabetically (from A to Z).

>>>Go Further

You can display additional details about the files you're viewing in File Explorer—and use those columns to arrange the file list—by clicking the Add Columns tool in the Current View group of the View tab.

When you click Add Columns, you'll see a check mark to the left of all the columns already included in the current view. For example, you might see checks in front of Date Modified, Type, Size, Tags, and Authors. Other items, such as Date Created, Categories, and Title, don't have checks. You can add them to your file display by clicking them. This enables you to show all files related to a particular topic, for example, or browse through files that were all created after a particular date.

You can click Choose Columns in the Add Columns list to add specific column items to your display. The long list of choices you'll see includes items such as Country/Region, Cell Phone, Contributors, Lens Model, Status, and much more. In this way, you can customize the look and feel of your File Explorer view so it gives you all the information you need about your files in a way that matches the way you like to work.

Copying, Moving, and Sharing Files and Folders

Some of the practical tasks you'll need to perform regularly with File Explorer involve copying, moving, and sharing your files. Copying can be as simple as selecting a file, pressing Ctrl+C, and then pressing Ctrl+V to paste the file in the folder in which you want it to appear. File Explorer helps ensure you're not copying over existing files by prompting you if a copy conflict occurs.

Copying Files

You can use the Copy To tool in the Organize group of the Home tab to copy one or many files in the selected folder.

1. In the Navigation pane, click or tap the folder containing the files you want to copy.

2. Select the files or folders you want to copy.

3. Click or tap the Home tab.

4. Click or tap Copy To. A list of copy destination appears

5. Click the folder where you want to paste the files. File Explorer immediately copies the selected files to the location you selected.

6. If you want to create a new folder or scroll through a list of possible folders, select the file you want to copy, click Copy To, and select Choose Location. The Copy Items dialog box appears.

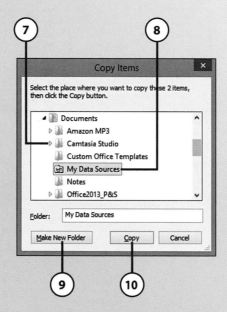

7. Click the arrow to display subfolders.

8. Click the folder where you want to copy the selected files.

9. Click Make New Folder if you want to copy the files to a new folder.

10. Click Copy to complete the operation.

Solving Copy Conflicts

When you inadvertently try to copy two files with the same name into the same location, File Explorer prompts you to resolve the conflict. This can happen easily when you are moving files from one computer to another—which file is the most recent one? File Explorer helps you make the call in the Replace or Skip Files dialog box.

1. Paste the files as usual in the new location. If files already exist in that folder with the same names, the Replace or Skip Files dialog box appears.

2. Click or tap Replace the File in the Destination if you want to replace the existing files with the ones you are pasting into the folder.

3. Click or tap Skip This File if you want to keep the existing file in the current folder.

4. If you want to compare the files, click or tap Compare Info for Both Files.

5. If you want to choose to keep the files in one of the folders displayed, click the check box to the left of your choice.

6. Compare the creation dates and times, as well as the file sizes, to determine which files you want to keep. Click or tap the check boxes of those files.

7. Click or tap Continue. File Explorer completes the copy operation using the file you selected.

Sharing Files

When you're ready to share your files with friends, family, and coworkers, select the file or group of files you want to share and tap or click the Share tab. You'll find tools that enable you to print, email, fax, burn to disc, or share the files with others in your HomeGroup or who have accounts on your computer.

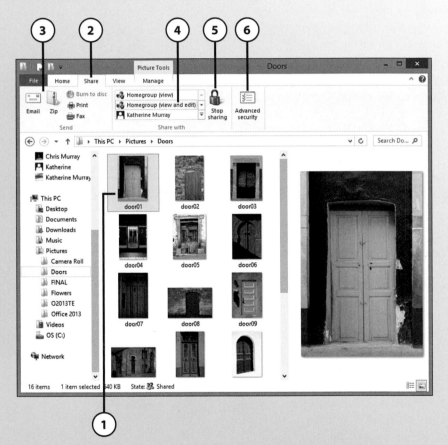

1. Select the file or files you want to share.

2. Click or tap the Share tab.

3. In the Send group, choose whether you want to Email, Zip, Burn to Disc, Print, or Fax your selection.

4. In the Share With group, select the groups or users from the list with whom you want to share the files.

5. If you want to stop sharing selected files, click Stop Sharing.

6. Fine-tune your security settings by clicking or tapping Advanced Security and adjusting the permission levels assigned to those you're sharing the files with.

Sync Your File Explorer Settings

When you select the Sync Your Settings tool in the PC Settings screen, you'll now be able to sync your File Explorer options and preferences along with the other Windows settings that are synced from computer to computer. This feature is available only if you log in to your computer using your Microsoft Account. Find out more about syncing your settings in Chapter 6, "Securing Your Computer."

Moving Files: Looks Familiar

Moving files is very similar to copying files. You simply navigate to the folder containing the files you want to move, select them, and click Move To in the Organize group of the Home tab. You'll see the trusty folder list, where you can select the destination folder where you want to move the files. Or you can click or tap Choose Location to display the Move Items dialog box, where you can choose a folder or subfolder—or add a new folder—you want to move the selected files to. Click Move to finish the job.

Copying and Moving Shortcut Keys

To use shortcut keys to copy and paste files, select the files you want to copy and press Ctrl+C. If you want to move the files instead of copying them, press Ctrl+X. Then, navigate to the folder where you want to place the copied or moved files, and press Ctrl+V.

Compressing and Extracting Your Files

Sometimes when you want to email a bunch of files, it's easier to compress them into one file you can attach to an email message instead of attaching 10 or 12 different documents. After the recipient receives the compressed file, he needs to extract the contents. File Explorer includes tools to do both of those jobs: compressing and extracting files.

1. Select the files you want to include in the compressed file.

2. Right-click your selection and point to Send To.

3. Click Compressed (Zipped) Folder. File Explorer compresses the files and displays the zipped file with the name highlighted.

4. Type a new name for the compressed file.

5. To see and extract the contents of a compressed file, double-click or double-tap it.

6. Click or tap Extract All. The Extract Compressed (Zipped) Folders dialog box appears.

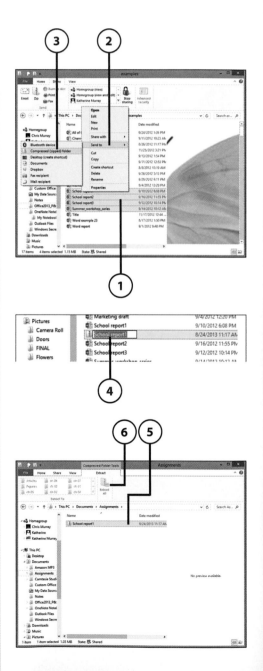

7. Click Browse if necessary to choose a folder for the extracted files. (It's okay to leave the default setting if that folder is where you want the uncompressed files to be placed.)

8. Click Extract. File Explorer extracts the files and places them in the folder you specified, ready to use.

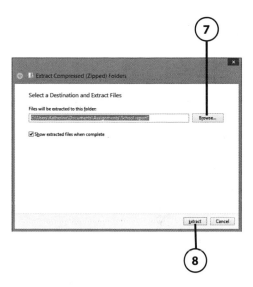

Extract Compressed (Zipped) Folders

Select a Destination and Extract Files

Files will be extracted to this folder:

S:\Users\Katherine\Documents\Assignments\School report\   Browse...

☑ Show extracted files when complete

Extract   Cancel

You can easily search
and browse in the
desktop version of IE11.

You can now choose
live tiles for your
Favorites in IE11.

In this chapter, you learn how to browse, read, and save web pages for later in Internet Explorer 11. Specifically, you learn how to use your web browser for the following tasks:

→ Introducing Internet Explorer 11
→ Browsing and searching the Web—the Windows way
→ Saving your favorites
→ Working with tabs
→ Securing your browsing experience

Browsing with Internet Explorer 11

The latest version of one of the world's most popular browsers includes some new features you'll enjoy if you like to save your favorite sites, work with multiple pages open at once, or read in-depth articles online. In addition to these visible and functional changes, Microsoft has improved performance, ensured faster page load times, and beefed up your security along the way.

Internet Explorer 11 still has that dual personality you might have heard about in IE 10 for Windows 8: One "modern" browser for the Start screen and another more traditional look for the desktop. That split still continues in IE 11. This chapter introduces you to Internet Explorer 11 no matter where you might choose to use it in Windows 8.1.

What's New in IE 11?

Internet Explorer 11, which is included with Windows 8.1 and Windows 8.1 RT, offers the most modern version of a Windows browser to date. New features include:

- **Better tools for your Favorites**—Favorites were all but left out of IE 10, and to save sites you wanted to return to later in your browser, you had to pin the site to your Start screen. Now in Windows 8.1, you have someplace specific (called, appropriately, Favorites) where you can save your favorite sites. And you can do some customizing along the way, too.

- **Unlimited tabs**—In IE 10, you could have up to 10 websites open at once, each in its own tab. Now in IE 11, you can have a virtually unlimited number of open tabs, which means you can switch among open pages to your heart's content.

- **Live tiles for your tabs**—Now when you add tabs to your Favorites center, you can opt whether to include live tiles for those sites that support it. Live tiles show you what the primary content on the site looks like, in a small thumbnail version.

- **Display tabs side-by-side**—In IE 11, you can snap tabs in place on your screen so that more than one webpage can be displayed at a time. This is great when you want to compare information or try to do two or more things at once.

- **Your preferences are synced**—If you signed in to Windows 8.1 using your Microsoft account, your Favorites, open tabs, and browser settings will be synced across all your Windows computers. This means that if you save your favorite news sites on your tablet, you'll be able to access them on your desktop PC, too, if you use your Microsoft account to log on.

Introducing Internet Explorer 11

Like everything else in Windows 8, Internet Explorer 11 works great on touchscreens, which means you can flick and tap and pinch to your heart's content. This touch interface lets you easily interact with the content you find: You can flick to another page, pinch to zoom in on a photo caption, and tap your way through navigation controls on the site.

The version of IE 11 you launch from your Start screen takes up your full Windows screen without displaying any kind of browser window. This full-screen experience is called "modeless" browsing because there's no bordering window with tools that enclose the browser window.

The desktop version of Internet Explorer 11 looks more like the traditional browsing experience you might be familiar with. You'll find the familiar browser window with tools you'll recognize as you surf the Web from the desktop. Whether you choose to go modeless or traditional, you'll find that IE 11 loads pages and updates faster than ever and provides the secure tools you need to have a safe browsing experience online.

>>>Go Further

ALL ABOUT PLUG-INS AND FLASH

A plug-in is a kind of utility that adds capabilities to your web browser. For example, Macromedia Flash is a plug-in that enables you to view animations in your web browser. Although plug-ins can add functionality to your browser, they also can be a security risk for your computer. For that reason, IE 11 on the Start screen is designed not to allow plug-ins of any kind, which makes for a smoother, faster, more secure browsing experience. But after some consideration, Microsoft added Adobe Flash support into IE 10 (and continues support in IE 11) so you can play media objects that require Flash. This is great when you're viewing video clips from news sites or You-Tube. But it's a bit ironic that Microsoft's own Silverlight is not supported by IE 11. You'll get bumped to the desktop version of the browser for that.

Starting Internet Explorer

By now you know the drill. Launch Internet Explorer 11 from your Start screen by tapping or clicking the Internet Explorer tile.

Tap or click to launch Internet Explorer 11 from the Start screen.

If you launch Internet Explorer 11 from your Windows 8.1 desktop, you'll click or tap the IE 11 logo on the left side of the taskbar.

Click or tap the IE 11 tool on the Desktop.

A Look Around the Internet Explorer Window(s)

No matter which browser you use, you'll find that each has its own unique personality with its own quirks and toolsets. It's not often, however, that you have two personalities in the same browser. Although Internet Explorer 11 is built on the same engine—meaning it processes information the same way and provides the same fast and efficient experience no matter which style you are using—it offers two very different browsing experiences.

IE 11: Modeless Style

No browser window—all web page, all the time

When you launch Internet Explorer 11 from the Start screen, the browser opens, displaying the webpage without a surrounding window, letting you easily touch, swipe, tap, right-click, and pinch your way across the Web.

To display additional pages, see the address bar, or work with your browser tools, you need to swipe up from the bottom of the browser window or right-click the mouse. The address bar appears at the bottom of the screen, along with navigation tiles of recently visited pages at the top of the screen.

Navigation tab—These thumbnail pages show where you've visited recently. You can move to one of the displayed pages by tapping or clicking it.

- **Back button**—Click or tap Back to move to the page you viewed immediately prior to the current page.

- **Address bar**—Tap or click in the address bar and enter the address of the webpage you want to view.

- **Refresh**—Update the display of the current page by tapping or clicking Refresh.

- **Favorites**—Tap or click this tool to display the Favorites bar, with any sites you've previously saved displayed so you can click them easily.

- **Tools**—You can tap or click Tools to open the page search feature so you can find content on the current page or choose to view the page on the desktop version of IE 11.

- **Forward**—Tap or click Forward to display the next page in a series of webpages. This tool is available only if you have previously used the Back button.

Switching to the Desktop Browser

If you're viewing a webpage in IE 11 and decide you'd rather have the traditional browser window instead, you can swipe up from the bottom of the browser window, tap or click Tools, and tap or click View on the Desktop. The IE 11 desktop browser window opens, with the current webpage displayed in the content area.

IE 11: Desktop Style

The desktop version of Internet Explorer 11, on the other hand, looks like a more traditional browser window, with the following elements that will probably look familiar:

- **One Box**—Now you can search for information or browse the Web by tapping or clicking and typing in the same box. Formerly called the address bar, One Box enables you to surf, search, refresh the site, and display security information all in the same box.

- **Page tab**—Each webpage is displayed in a separate tab, and the tabs are color-coded to help you navigate among them easily.

- **Home**—Clicking Home at any point returns you to the website you've set as your browser homepage.

- **View Favorites**—Click View Favorites to access websites you've saved as your favorites or to add a new favorite to the list.

- **Tools**—Click Tools to access the various menus in Internet Explorer 11 and to print, check site security, go to your pinned sites, and set Internet options.

Making the Menus Visible

In the desktop version of IE 11, you can display traditional menus at the top of the browser window if you like. Simply press Alt, and the menus (File, Edit, View, Favorites, Tools, and Help) appear just below One Box, where you can reach them easily.

Browsing and Searching the Web

If you are a smartphone user, chances are you're already browsing the Web using a touch interface, so IE 11 might feel very natural to you. The version of IE 11 you launch from the Start screen enables you to tap or click your way from page to page easily. You can also swipe to advance pages, zoom in on content, and dock the display so you can view the Web alongside other open apps. Sweet.

Using the Address Bar

The address bar appears when you first display a webpage and reappears when you swipe up from the bottom of the IE 11 screen. To anchor the cursor in the address bar, you tap or click there. As you type in the address bar, the navigation tiles filter to show you sites from your history, favorites, and even popular URLs. With Windows 8 roaming and connected accounts, your browsing history and favorites roam with you

so you can easily access recent webpages across all of your PCs.

1. Click or tap in the address bar. If
   you're using a touch device, the
   touch keyboard appears so you
   can type the new web address.
   If you're using a non-touch
   computer, the web address is
   highlighted.

2. Type the web address of
   the page you want to view.
   Internet Explorer 11 attempts
   to autocomplete the phrase for
   you, so if you want to use the
   site provided, tap or click the Go
   button. If not, just keep typing the
   full address.

3. You can also tap or click a tile in
   the Suggestions area to move to
   the page in IE 11.

4. If you're using the desktop
   version, IE 11 offers suggested
   sites in a drop-down list when you
   begin to type the web address,
   and you can tap or click the site
   you want to display.

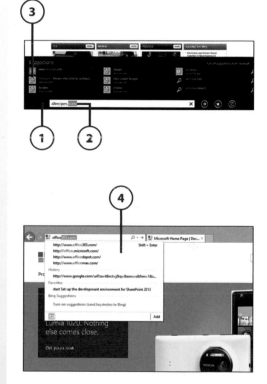

What's in a Name?

In the desktop version of IE 11,
the address bar is known as One
Box, where you now basically use
"one box" for everything, whether
you want to search, get security
reports, or go directly to a webpage.

KEYBOARD SHORTCUTS FOR BROWSING

If you'd rather skip the clicking and navigate through the Web using your keyboard, you can use the following shortcut keys in the desktop version of IE 11:

- Press Alt+C to display your favorites, feeds, and history.

- Press Ctrl+B to organize your favorites.

- Press Ctrl+D to add another webpage to your favorites.

- Press Ctrl+L to highlight the web address in One Box. (This also works in the version of IE 11 you launch from the Start screen.)

- Press Ctrl+J to display the Download Manager.

Navigating the Web

The Web has been around long enough by now that you probably won't be surprised by the browser tools you'll use to navigate online. Whether you're using IE 11 from the Start screen or desktop, chances are good you already know how to move forward or backward from page to page.

In both browsers, you'll use the same tools and techniques to navigate the webpages you display:

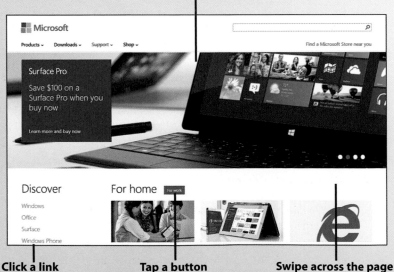

IE 11 modern browser

Click a link **Tap a button** **Swipe across the page**

Forward   **IE 11 desktop browser**

Back

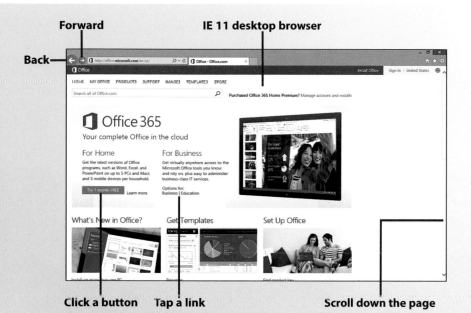

Click a button   Tap a link   Scroll down the page

- **Back**—Tapping or clicking the Back button takes you back to the page you were previously viewing.

- **Forward**—Tapping or clicking Forward takes you to the webpage you previously viewed after viewing the current one. This capability is helpful if you're moving back and forth between pages. If you haven't moved ahead to another page yet, this button is not available for you to click or tap.

- **Click or tap a link**—Click or tap a link on the page to move to another page or perform a web action. What that link does—for example, whether it displays a new page, opens a document, or plays a media clip—depends on what the website designer programmed the link to do.

- **Scroll or swipe down the page**—In the desktop version of IE 11, use the vertical scrollbar as you would in any other program to display content that is currently out of view along the bottom of the page. On a touch device, you can swipe up to display content that appears below the bottom margin of the window.

- **Scroll or swipe across the page**—In the desktop version of IE 11, use the horizontal scrollbar to scroll across pages that are too wide to be displayed at one time on your monitor. Using the version of IE 11 you launch from the Start screen, you can swipe to the left to show content that is out of view to the right. You can also swipe to the right or left to page through other webpages you've visited.

- **Tap or click a tool or command**—You can carry out site operations, execute commands, and access other areas of the site by tapping or clicking a button, command, or menu item.

PIN YOUR SITES WHERE YOU CAN FIND THEM LATER

>>>Go Further

If you use some sites often, you can pin them to the Start screen so you can go to them directly with a single tap or click.

To pin a site to the Start screen, tap the IE 11 tile on the Start screen and navigate to the site you want to add, swipe up to display the address bar, and tap the Favorites tool (which looks like a star). Then tap Pin to Start (which resembles a push pin). This displays a pop-up box in which you can choose the look of the tile you want to use (click the arrows on either site of the logo image); tap Pin to Start to finalize the deal. Now you'll be able to go this site directly without first opening Internet Explorer.

Saving Your Favorites

Pinning sites to the Start screen is a nice option to have, but if you're like many of us, you don't want to have a gazillion tiles on the Start screen you have to swipe through. In the previous version of Internet Explorer (version 10), Favorites were dramatically underplayed. Now they are back in Internet Explorer 11 and, what's more, they are flexible and easy to use.

Adding a Favorite

You can easily add a favorite site to your Favorites list in IE 11. When you add the site to your list, you can also change the name of the site and even choose a live tile, if one is available for that particular offering.

1. Display IE 11 from the Start screen and navigate to the webpage you want to add as a favorite.

2. Tap or click the Favorites tool.

3. Tap or click Add to Favorites.

4. Click in the title box, and type a name for the Favorite if you like.

5. Tap or click in the locations box; then choose where you want to save the favorite.

6. Click the tile image arrow to display images you can choose for the live tile.

7. Tap or click Add.

Live Tiles for Your Favorites

The pinned websites in IE 10 were pretty drab, but now, if site developers have programmed this feature into their sites, you can choose the live image you want to appear as the tile for the Favorites site. You'll be able to get a small thumbnail view of the live tiles before you even open the webpage in IE11.

WHO SAYS YOU CAN'T GO BACK?

>>>Go Further

Internet Explorer 11 makes it easy to return to sites you browsed earlier—or go back to your last browsing session. If you're using the modeless version of IE 11, swipe up to display the address bar at the bottom and the navigation tiles at the top of your browser screen. Tap or click the tile you want to view.

If you're using the desktop version of IE 11, click the New Tab box to the right of the last tab open in your browsing window, and, if you want to revisit earlier sites, click Reopen Closed Tabs (on the bottom left). A list of sites you visited earlier appears. Just click the site you want to display.

If you want to return to your last browsing session, click the Reopen Last Session link. Internet Explorer automatically opens the webpage you were visiting the last time you used the browser.

Using Navigation Tiles

The modeless version of Internet Explorer 11 employs colorful tiles—similar to those you see on the Windows 8.1 Start screen—to help you move to your favorite and most frequently visited sites. These tiles appear when you swipe up from the bottom of the IE 11 screen or when you tap or click in the address bar.

1. Swipe up from the bottom of the screen. The address bar appears along the bottom, and the open page appears as a navigation tile just above that.

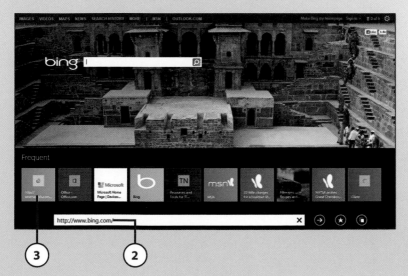

2. Tap or click in the address bar. The screen displays a list of tiles, showing your most recently visited sites. On the left are the 10 most frequently visited sites, and on the right, IE 11 lists any sites you've pinned to the Start screen. Note that if you tap in the address bar, the onscreen keyboard will also appear, but if you click in the address bar, only the navigation tiles will be shown.

3. Tap or click the tile of the page you want to display, and the webpage opens and fills the screen.

Searching for Information

If you're like many of us, you probably spend quite a bit of time with search engines. I typically start my day searching for something or other in Google or Bing. (I'm using Bing more and more lately because I love the photos they use as the search background.) If you use the version of IE 11 you launch from the Start screen, you can also use the Windows 8.1 Search charm to find what you're looking for and the browser will automatically scour the Web for you.

With the desktop version of IE 11, you can just tap or click in One Box and type what you're looking for; that functions as a search box, too. Both techniques are simple and will get you to the information you're looking for.

Searching in IE 11 from the Start Screen

Searching is fast and easy in IE 11. You don't even need to open the browser if you don't want to. You could display the Search charm, type what you want to find, and tap Internet Explorer. Or, if the browser's already open, just enter the search text in the box and you're good to go.

1. In IE 11, swipe in from the right to display the Charms bar.

2. Tap or click Search.

3. Tap or click in the Search box and begin to type a word or phrase that reflects what you're searching for. If you tap, Windows 8.1 displays the onscreen keyboard. As you type, Windows displays a number of possible search phrases that include the letters you've entered.

4. To choose one of the suggested search phrases, tap or click it.

5. To search for the word or phrase you entered, tap the Search tool. The results appear in a Bing window on the left side of your screen, and you can tap or click a link that you think will have the information you seek.

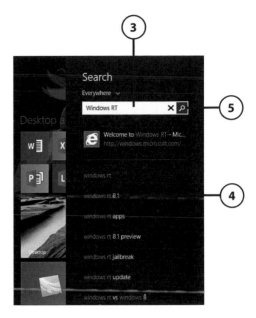

Browse, Shop, It's All the Same

One cool feature that we're sure to see more of in the modern version of IE 11 is the connection to the Windows Store. When a site you visit also has an app available that you can download to use with Windows, you will be able to click or tap the site icon to the left of the address bar to download the app automatically. Pretty slick!

Searching in IE 11 Desktop

In the desktop version of IE 11, you can click in One Box and type a word or phrase that describes what you'd like to find—for example, entering "badminton" brings suggestions like badminton rules, badminton rackets, and badminton history. Bing is the default search engine Microsoft uses to display a list of suggestions related to your search; you can click the suggestion you like to narrow your search and display a page of results with links to webpages you might want to visit.

1. Click or tap in One Box and type a word or phrase describing what you want to find.

2. Your search provider—which is Bing until you tell IE 11 otherwise—displays a list of search results, ranked from those that match your search phrase most closely to those that are not as close a match. Click or tap a link you'd like to view.

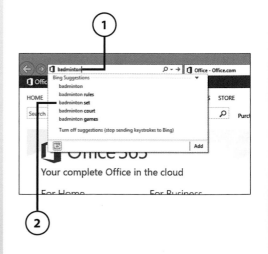

TURNING ON SUGGESTIONS

You won't see search suggestions in your IE 11 desktop browser if you haven't turned on suggestions so that Bing can do the searching for you. To turn on this feature, type the word or phrase you're looking for in the One Box at the top of the IE 11 desktop window. In the drop-down area, click or tap Turn On Suggestions (Send Keystrokes to Bing). Bing will then send the search text you entered and you'll see a list of search categories. Tap or click the one that reflects what you're looking for.

You can turn off this feature at any time by clicking or tapping Turn Off Suggestions, which appears at the bottom of the search list.

Adding Search Providers

You can add search provides to the desktop version of IE 11 so that your search goes out far and wide through your favorite search engines. After you type your search word in One Box, click or tap Add at the bottom of the results list. You are taken online to the Internet Explorer Gallery, where you can select an add-on for a search provider you'd like to include with IE 11. Note that even though the Windows 8.1 version of IE 11 doesn't support add-ons, the desktop version of IE 11 does.

Selecting Your Home Page

The version of IE 11 you launch from the Start screen doesn't give you an option of setting a home page. Rather, the page displayed in the browser by default is the last page you used the browser to view.

You can set a home page in IE 11 for the desktop, however. You'll find the tools you need in the Home Page area of the General tab in the Internet Options dialog box.

1. In the desktop version of IE 11, display the page you want to use as your home page.

2. Click or tap the Tools icon.

3. Select Internet Options.

4. In the Home Page area of the General tab, tap or click Use Current.

5. Select OK. Now whenever you launch IE 11, the browser opens to the webpage you specified.

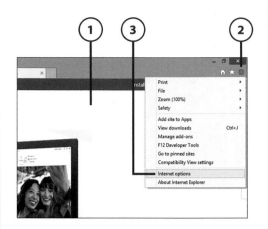

Multiple Home Pages

If you have several sites you like to check first thing in the morning, you can add them all to the Home Page area of the General tab in the Internet Options dialog box in IE 11 for the desktop. Simply put each web address on its own line and then select OK. When you launch the desktop version of IE 11 the next time, all the webpages you entered will open automatically.

Working with Tabs

Once upon a time, web browsers allowed us to have only one webpage open at a time, but today we're able to have multiple pages open in different tabs in Internet Explorer. The desktop version of IE 11 shows each individual tab across the top of the browser window, but the modern version of IE 11 displays tabs as navigation tiles, which are thumbnails of the open pages, displayed at the top of your browser screen.

Windows 8.1 increases the limit on the number of tabs you can have open at once to a virtually unlimited number. In fact, you can have up to 100 active tabs in each browser window (try to keep all *those* pages straight!).

Using Tabs in IE 11

Tabs in the modern version of IE 11 don't look like tabs in the desktop version of IE 11. In fact, they don't look like tabs at all. When you want to display the collection of webpages you already have open, you can swipe down from the top of the screen or up from the bottom. You can also press Windows+Z or right-click the mouse to display your IE 11 tabs.

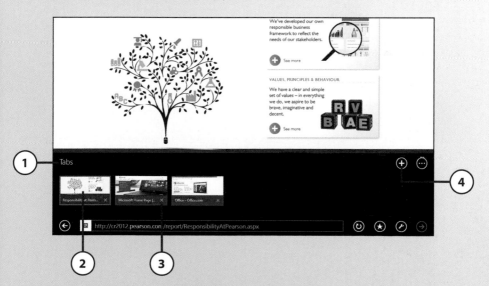

1. Swipe down from the top of the IE 11 browser window. The tab thumbnails appear.
2. To move to a specific tab, tap or click it. The page appears full-screen.
3. To close a tab you no longer want to use, tap or click the Close button.
4. To add a tab, click or tap the Add Tab button.

Displaying Tabs Side by Side

If your browser window has a resolution high enough, you can display more than one webpage on your screen at a time. This enables you to switch back and forth between items while you're shopping or playing a game (or updating social media) while you're checking the latest headlines.

The process is simple: Snap the tab to the portion of the screen you want it to occupy, and then right-click a link and tell Windows to display the new link in a new window. The pages appear side-by-side on your screen.

1. Snap the first tab to the portion of the screen where you want it to appear.

2. Right-click the link you want to open. An options list appears.

3. Tap or click Open Link in a New Window. Internet Explorer 11 displays the new page in the blank area of the screen.

4. Change the size of the tabs, if you like, by dragging the divider bar between the tab windows.

QUIET SURFING WITH INPRIVATE BROWSING

In some cases, you might not want to track your browsing activity for others to see. Perhaps you're shopping for a holiday gift for someone and you don't want him to inadvertently discover it. You can turn on InPrivate Browsing to tell Internet Explorer 11 to skip recording your web activity. This means that the sites you visit won't be available in your browsing history, cookies, form data, temporary Internet files, or the usernames and passwords Internet Explorer 11 usually keeps.

You can turn on InPrivate Browsing two different ways (surprise, surprise). In the modern version of IE 11, display the tabs by swiping down from the top of the screen and tap or click the Tab Tools button; then click or tap New InPrivate Tab. If you're using the desktop version of IE 11, tap or click the Tools icon in the upper-right area of browser window. Click or tap Safety, and then select InPrivate Browsing. Or, if you prefer the shortcut key, press Ctrl+Shift+P to launch InPrivate browsing. Internet Explorer 11 opens a new browser session independent of the current one you have been using, and none of your browsing information is stored in the new session. When you're ready to end the InPrivate Browsing session, simply close the browser session.

Opening a New Tab in Desktop IE 11

The process of opening a tab in the desktop version of IE 11 is probably familiar. This enables you to view another webpage in addition to the one—or ones—you're already viewing.

1. In the desktop version of IE 11, click or tap the New Tab button to the right of the current tab.

2. In the New Tab page, you can see site panels of the most recently viewed websites you've visited. You can tap or click one of the panels to go to that page.

3. You can also use the One Box to type the web address of the site you want to visit. Alternatively, you can enter a word or phrase and search for the content you want to find.

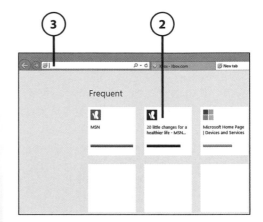

Double-Display Duty

You can view two or more pages at the same time in the desktop version of IE 11 by tapping and holding or clicking a tab and dragging it toward the center of the browser window. The page comes "undocked" from the browser window, and you can position it onscreen wherever you want it by tapping and holding or clicking and then dragging the top of the window.

Securing Your Browsing Experience

Internet Explorer 11 includes additional security issues that help Microsoft catch any threats before they are downloaded to your browser window. IE also offers all kinds of security technologies, such as SmartScreen, Application Reputation, InPrivate browsing, Tracking Protection, and hang detection and recovery. The modern version of IE 11 doesn't use add-ons, which can sometimes introduce security risks, although you are still able to use add-ons with the desktop version of IE 11.

Enhanced Protected mode isolates the website content that appears in each tab. And InPrivate browsing is also segregated per tab, so your browsing is more secure and private than ever.

WHAT'S ALL THE FUSS ABOUT DO NOT TRACK?

Another security measure included with Windows 8.1 is the Do Not Track feature, which was initially enabled by default (but was disabled in the release version of Windows 8). Do Not Track is a setting that tells webpages you visit that you have opted not to have your browsing habits recorded. This is a good thing for consumer privacy (and the U.S. administration is pushing for this type of safeguard to enhance user safety), but online advertisers who sell ads based on traffic statistics and user browsing data are up in arms about the possibility.

To turn on the Do Not Track feature in your version of Internet Explorer 11, click or tap Tools in IE 11 desktop, select Internet Options, and select the Advanced tab. Scroll down to the Security area and click to add a check mark to the Send Do Not Track Requests to Sites You Visit in Internet Explorer check box. Click OK. After you make the change, you'll need to restart your computer to put the new setting into effect. But you'll have the comfort of knowing that at least your data isn't helping to sell goods to unsuspecting consumers.

Deleting Cookies

It's a good idea in the desktop version of IE 11 to regularly clean off the cookies that have accumulated on your computer, both to keep their drain on your computer's memory low and to clean out any potentially sneaky cookies that could be sending information back to the site that placed them.

1. In the desktop version of IE 11, tap or click Tools. The Tools list appears.

2. Point to Safety.

3. Select Delete Browsing History. The Delete Browsing History dialog box appears.

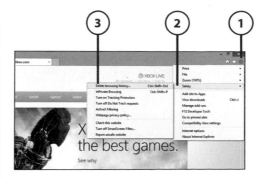

4. The first item in the dialog box, Preserve Favorites Website Data, retains information—cookies and all—related to sites you have marked as Favorites. In most cases, you should leave this item selected.

5. Review the list of checked and unchecked items. The checked items are deleted; the unchecked items are not. Change the items as needed to suit your preference. You might, for example, want to delete all the form data you have entered in online forms; if so, check the Form Data check box.

6. Click or tap Delete to delete the cookies and other information you've selected.

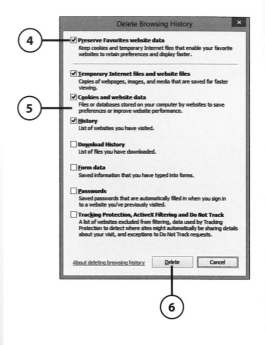

SO WHAT ARE COOKIES, ANYWAY?

>>>Go Further

The websites you visit want you to come back (and buy something—from them or one of their advertisers), so they want you to have a personalized experience on their site. This means they want to make visiting their site a pleasant experience for you, so they save information about your time on the site—your preferences and your username and password if you created them—in what's known as a *cookie*; the cookie is stored on your computer. Then, whenever you return to that site, your preferences are there to personalize your web experience with the items you said you like. Pretty clever, right?

But some cookies can do more than save your preferences. They also can track your web activities, and that borders on infringing upon your privacy. In Internet Explorer 11, you can control the cookies stored on your computer by deleting them, limiting them, or blocking all of them.

The People app makes
it easy to keep up with
friends and family.

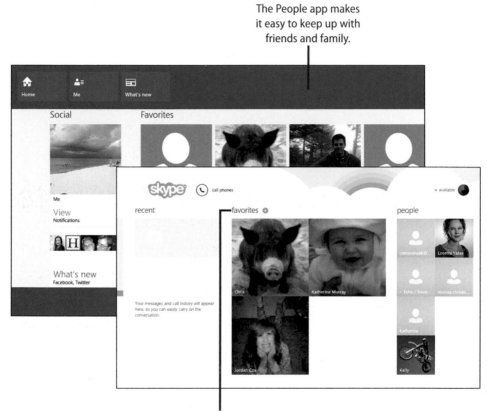

You can now add favorites
to Skype so you can reach
your contact easily.

In this chapter, you learn to use Skype, the People app, and the Mail and Calendar apps to keep your connection strong with these tasks:

→ Calling and messaging with Skype

→ Getting social with the People app

→ Staying in touch through email

→ Keeping your dates straight with the Calendar app

Connect and Communicate with Windows 8.1

If you think about what you use your computer and your devices to do most often, chances are good that at least a few of those top tasks involve communicating with people in some way. Perhaps you send a lot of email messages; schedule appointments on your calendar; call friends, family, and clients; or catch up on your favorite social media accounts.

People—and our interactions with them—are central to all we do.

Windows 8.1 includes a number of built-in tools that enables you to stay in touch with others. This latest version of Windows has updates to several of the apps you'll use to communicate and connect. Now Skype is included as part of Windows 8.1 and is not something you have to download and install separately. Skype also now serves as the app you use when you want to send instant messages to others, which means the Messaging app that was part of Windows 8 proper is now gone. The People app has had a few feature tweaks that make connecting with contacts easier and more intuitive, too.

This chapter shines a light on the tools you'll use to stay in touch with those near and far using Windows 8.1.

Calling and Messaging with Skype

Skype was acquired by Microsoft fairly recently, and the software developer has been working on plans to integrate Skype—which offers video and voice calling, as well as instant messaging—into all sorts of Microsoft products. Skype is now a regular part of Windows 8.1, and you'll also find Skype capability in Office products and, perhaps most logically, Outlook.

Launching Skype

You'll find the Skype app tile on your Start screen, and to launch the program you only need to tap or click it. The Skype window displays your most recent activity, along with your Skype favorites and other contacts.

1. Tap or click the Skype app tile on the Start screen. The Skype window opens.

2. Review any recent activity in the account.

3. Scroll to the right to find the contact you want to call or message.

Receive Calls Anytime

Even if you've set your Skype availability to Invisible, the calls will still come through in Windows 8.1. You'll get a notification about the incoming call and, if you miss it, a Skype notification icon will appear on your Lock screen, letting you know how many calls you've missed.

Adding Skype Contacts

In a perfect world (and maybe this is coming), the People app in Windows 8.1 would automatically integrate Skype usernames so that anyone available in your People list would also be available for a Skype call. At this point in time, though, that isn't possible, so you need to add your Skype contacts to the app before they are available for calling or messaging. Here's how.

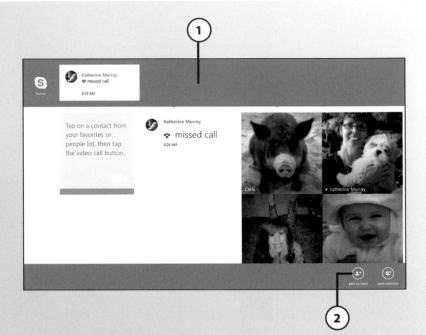

1. In the Skype window, swipe up or right-click the screen. The app options bar appears.

2. Tap or click Add Contact. The Skype search panel appears.

3. Type the first few characters of the Skype username you want to find.

4. Click or tap the Search tool. The results page displays Skype users who meet your search criteria.

5. Tap or click the contact you want to add.

6. If the result you want isn't displayed, click Search Directory to search for the Skype user you want. Scroll through the displayed list and tap the user you want to add.

7. In the Skype user screen, tap or click Add to Contacts. A pop-up contact request box appears.

8. Type a note for the contact, asking his permission to add him to your Skype contact list.

9. Click Send. When the user accepts your contact request, he will appear in your Skype contacts and you'll be able to call and message your new contact.

Making a Call with Skype

After you have your contacts set in Skype, calling is easy. You can choose whether you want to make a video call, make an audio call, or send a text message, all with a simple click or tap.

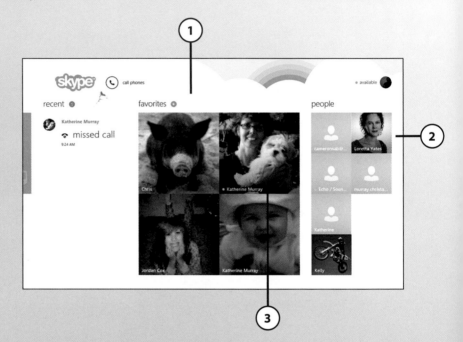

1. Display the Skype window.

2. Scroll to the right if necessary to see additional contacts.

3. Tap or click the contact you want to call. The contact screen opens, showing your history of communication with that person and giving you options for contact.

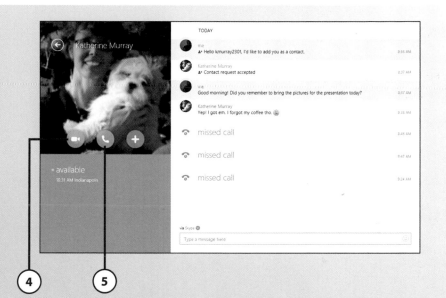

4. Click or tap to open a video call.

5. Click or tap to begin an audio call.

Video is turned on   Audio is turned on   Display Skype options

6. Skype displays the call window.

7. If you are making a video call, the video appears in the profile area in the center of the screen. If your contact does not have video capability, her profile picture appears there instead.

8. When you're ready to end the call, click End.

How Do I Contact Thee? Let Me Count the Ways

The question of whether your contact is online when you're trying to contact her makes a difference in the number of tools you'll see in the contact window. If your contact is not online, you'll see only the green video call and audio call buttons in the upper-left corner of the screen, at the bottom of the contact's profile picture. If the contact is online, a blue button appears that enables you to add and send files, send a video message, or add participants to the call.

Answering a Call with Skype

Before someone can call you using Skype, you must already have accepted his contact request, so you shouldn't be getting Skype calls from lots of telemarketers you've never met (which is a good thing). When you receive a call on Skype, a notification appears and a sound plays to let you know a call is coming in. You can, of course, choose to answer the call—or not.

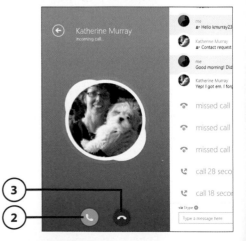

1. When a Skype notification appears in the upper-right corner of your screen, tap it to open the Skype window.

2. Click or tap to answer the call. The Skype window opens and you can continue the call as normal.

3. Click or tap Hangup to end the call.

It's Not All Good

SKYPE UNDERDELIVERS ON THE LOCK SCREEN SO FAR

Microsoft is saying that you can receive calls and use Skype without even unlocking your computer, but here's how it works on my computer so far. When my lock screen is displayed, a call notification appears in the upper-right corner and a chime sounds to let me know a call is coming in. When I tap the notification, however, it doesn't answer the call; it just bumps the lock screen image (which seems to want to scroll up). I need to unlock the computer with my pin before I can answer the call (and anyone who is calling me is almost sure to hang up in the time it takes me to do that).

Skype does then display missed call notifications at the bottom of the lock screen, which is a good thing because I'm sure to miss a few calls until they get this "seamless integration" smoothed out.

Sending Messages

Now that Skype is a live-in part of Windows 8.1, the messaging aspect of Skype completely fills the bill for any instant messaging needs you might have. You can send messages easily through Skype and the app keeps track of the communication for you.

1. Display the contact to which you want to send the message, click or tap in the message box, and type your message.

2. Click or tap to add an emoticon if you like, and then press Enter to send the message.

Choosing Your Messaging Service

The messaging service Skype displays just above the message box will vary, depending on the source of the contact you've selected. If your contact is from the list compiled in the previous Messaging app, the selection might say "via Messaging." If you click the down arrow and select SMS Mobile, Skype will prompt you to buy Skype credits for sending SMS messages.

Getting Social with the People App

The People app brings together all your contacts from your various social media accounts and displays them all in one lovely alphabetical list, ready for you to tap or click to contact. You can find out what's going on with a specific contact, get a news feed of status updates, and view or update your own social media information.

Getting Started with the People App

You'll find the People app toward the left of the Windows 8 Start screen. If you've moved your tiles around, as described in Chapter 3, "Using and Tweaking the Start Screen," you might have to do a little scrolling to find your People app. You'll recognize your People app by the pictures of friends and family members that make up the surface of the tile.

1. On the Start screen, tap the People app. The People screen appears, giving you a number of choices for the way you work with contacts and profile information.

2. Tap or click Me to display your profile information and recent updates.

3. Click or tap See All Notifications to see how others have interacted with your posts and updates.

4. Tap a contact to view all the ways you can contact that individual.

5. Swipe up from the bottom or down from the top of the screen to display the apps bar.

6. Click or tap Me to see your profile and review your own posts to social media.

7. Click or tap What's New to see updates from all the social media accounts you've connected to the People app.

Updating Your Profile Info

What you post in your profile—and whom you share it with—is your call. Your social media accounts and Windows 8.1 don't need access to your contact information, location, or interests to function properly. You can set the permissions on your profile so it can be seen by only you, some friends, all friends, your friends and their friends, or everyone. To change the permissions on your profile, click the link to the right of Shared With in your profile information online.

Connecting Your Social Media Accounts

You can connect Windows 8.1—and specifically, the People app—to as many or as few social media accounts as you'd like. The People app shows you which accounts are connected and gives you an easy way to make changes as needed.

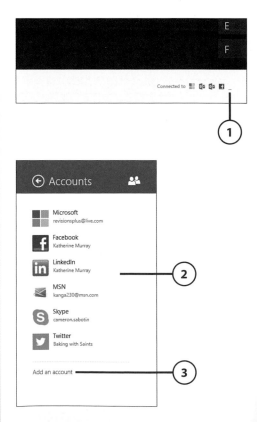

1. In the People app, tap or click the dots to the right of the Connected To line at the bottom-right corner of the People app. The Accounts panel opens, showing your current account connections.

2. Review all the accounts listed.

3. Click the Add an Account link.

4. In the Add an Account area, tap the account you'd like to connect to your People app.

5. Enter your email address.

6. Type your password.

7. Click or tap Connect.

Vive la Difference

Depending on the account you choose to add to your People app, the process for connecting it to Windows 8.1 might be slightly different. You will be asked for your email address or login and password, and you might be asked to confirm that you're giving permission for this app to access your computer. In any case, the process is simple, and you should be up and running in just a matter of minutes.

Getting a New Facebook Account

If you don't currently have a Facebook account, you can create one at this point. Click or tap the Sign Up for Facebook link at the bottom of the Connecting to a Service screen. Facebook will walk you through the process of creating a new account that you can link to your People app.

>>>Go Further

WHAT WILL I BE ABLE TO SEE?

Different social media apps allow you to do different types of things in the People app (they're all somewhat different, after all). Here's a quick list of what you'll be able to do with some of the main social media apps in Windows 8.1:

- When you connect to Facebook, you'll be able to chat with your Facebook friends from within Windows 8.1, update your Facebook status, and share documents and photos with your Facebook friends. You'll also be able to view in Windows 8.1 the photos you upload to your Facebook account.

- When you connect to Twitter, you'll be able to post new tweets, read tweets from your timeline as you would in Twitter, view the people you follow, choose to follow new people, and update your Twitter profile. You won't be able to see any direct messages you receive or view your Twitter password.

- With LinkedIn, you'll be able to update your LinkedIn status, share documents and photos, and view your LinkedIn contacts.

You can also add accounts from Hotmail, Outlook, and Google to your People app to make the most of all your online contacts and reach all your friends and family through a single, organized app.

Viewing Status Updates

The great thing about the People app is that it can give you up-to-the-minute updates on friends and family no matter which social media site they might be using. This means you can see Facebook updates, tweets, and more, all in one handy display.

1. Display the People app, and swipe up or down (or right-click) to display the apps bar.

2. Tap or click What's New. The updates are listed with the most recent updates on the left.

3. Scroll or swipe to the right to display status updates from all your connected social media accounts.

4. Choose whether you want to add the post to your favorites, retweet it, or reply to it.

5. Click or tap an update you want to read more about. The post opens full-screen.

6. Tap or click to Like the post.

7. Click or tap Add a Comment to enter a comment, and then press Enter.

Responding to Posts, Tweets, and More

The actions that are available after you click or tap a social media update one of your contacts has posted will depend, of course, on the social media account she's using. If you tap an update from Facebook, you can Like or comment on the post. If you tap an update from Twitter, you can add it to your Favorites, retweet it, or respond to the tweet.

It's Not All Good

TOO MANY UPDATES!

If you find yourself drowning in status updates and you're not really seeing the ones you want to see, you can have the People app filter the updates for you. Tap or click the down arrow to the right of the What's New heading in the upper-left corner of the page. Then select the social media account you want to see, which limits the number of updates displayed in the What's New screen.

Adding a New Contact

You can easily add a new contact to the People app, which then makes that person available in your Mail app, too.

1. Launch the People app.

2. Swipe up from the bottom or right-click near the bottom of the screen. The apps bar appears.

3. Tap or click New Contact.

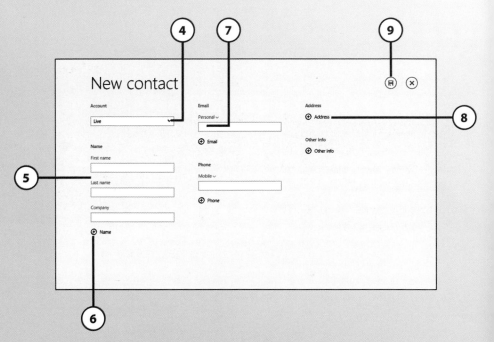

4. Choose the account for the contact by clicking or tapping the arrow and selecting your choice.

5. Enter the first name and last name of the contact.

6. If you want to add more information—such as the phonetic spelling of the first name—tap or click the Name control to see a list of fields you can add.

7. Enter the email address for the new contact.

8. Add Address information if you like.

9. Tap or click Save to save the new contact to your Peoples app.

Searching for a Contact

If you're having a hard time finding someone in your contact list by scrolling through the list (that's part of the price you pay for being so popular), you can easily search for the contact in the People app.

1. Launch the People app on your Start screen.

2. Type the first name of the person you want to find. The Search panel appears and the letters you type are in the search box.

3. Tap or click Search.

4. Choose the contact in the results list you were looking for.

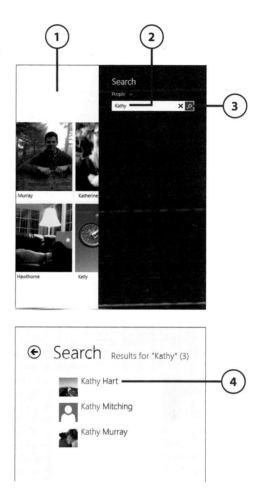

Staying in Touch Through Email

Email is included as a part of your operating system, thanks to the Mail app in Windows 8.1. The Mail app is simplified and straightforward, and you can read, respond, and manage your email easily, whether you're using a touch-based system or the mouse and keyboard to get around.

The new design in Windows 8.1 displays icons along the left side of the Mail app window so that you can click or tap the types of messages you want to see. You can view your Inbox as usual or choose Social Updates to see what your friends are up to, Newsletters to read through your latest newsletters, or Flagged to see the messages you've flagged for follow-up later.

Adding an Email Account

First, you need to let Windows 8.1 know about your email account so that you can download and respond to the messages you receive. When you first installed and launched Windows 8.1, Windows asked you for your Microsoft Account, so chances are that at least that web-based email account is already activated in your Mail hub. You can add other accounts, too, so you receive the messages that really matter, whether you are sitting in your office or are out and about in the world.

1. Tap Mail in the Start screen to display the Mail app.

2. Swipe in from the right or move the mouse to the right side of the screen to display the Charms bar.

3. Tap or click Settings.

4. Click or tap Accounts.

5. Tap or click Add an Account.

6. Click or tap the account type you want to add.

7. Enter your email address.

8. Type your password.

9. Click Connect.

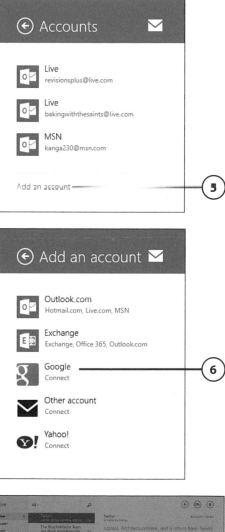

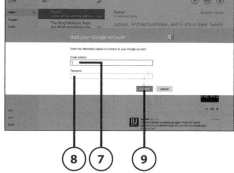

CHANGING ACCOUNT SETTINGS

You can tweak the settings of your email account to specify how often you want to check for new content, which types of information you want to download, and whether the account shows notifications on your Windows desktop or Lock screen. You can also remove the account if you like.

Display the Mail app window and tap the account you want to modify in the left column of the Mail window. Swipe in or click the right side of the screen to display the Charms bar; tap Settings. Tap or click Accounts, and then tap the account you want to change. You can modify the account name, let Windows know when you want to download content, and choose the items you want to sync (you can select Sync, Contacts, or Calendar). You can change notifications by sliding the Show Notifications for This Account from Off to On.

When you want to return to the Mail app, simply click outside the settings area and it closes.

Checking Out the Mail Window

The Mail app presents a streamlined, easy-to-navigate screen that enables you to review your mail quickly, click the message you want to read through, organize your mail into folders, and respond easily to the message at hand.

The icons along the left side of the Mail window enable you to display just the messages you want to view. You can display your favorites, review the results of past searches, see your flagged messages, read through the newsletters you receive, catch up on social media updates, or view the contents of the mail folders you create.

Click an icon to display messages

Selected message

Respond to the current message

Create new message

Delete selected message

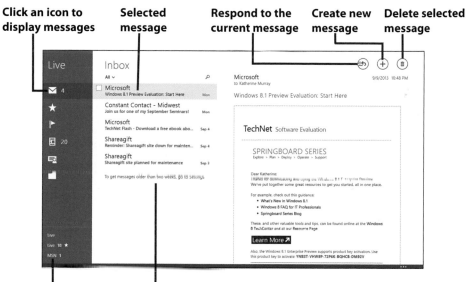

Choose an email account to view

Messages in the selected folder

Composing an Email Message

When you're ready to create a new email message, the task is simple. Tap or click the New icon in the upper-right corner of the Mail window, and a blank message opens. You can then choose the contact you want to send the message to, add a subject line, and compose the message you want to send. You can also attach files, insert pictures, and more. Here's how:

1. In the Mail app window, tap or click New.

2. Click or tap in the To box and begin to type the contact's name. The names of individuals in your People app appear; you can click to select the name you want to use.

3. Click in the Add a Subject line and type a message subject.

4. Click in the message area and type your message.

5. Click Show More to add a blind copy line, to set the priority of the message, or to send the message from a different account.

6. Click Attachments if you want to add a file to the message. Choose the file from the screen that appears.

7. Click Send to send the message.

8. Or, click Discard to delete the message without sending it.

Organizing Your Email

If you're like most of us, you receive dozens—if not hundreds—of messages each day that you have to decide what to do with. Some might be junk mail; others might be notices that don't really apply to you. Others are messages you need to keep—perhaps notes about upcoming meetings, or deadlines, or fun plans. You can organize your mail by filing it away in folders you create, or you can pin a message to your task list so you'll remember to follow up on it sooner rather than later.

1. In the Mail app, open the message you want to file.

2. Swipe up or right-click the bottom of the screen. The Mail app options appear.

3. Tap or click Manage Folders.

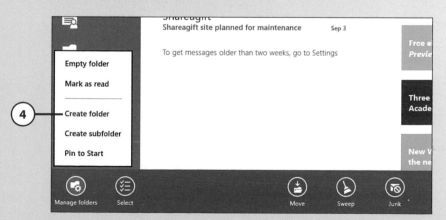

4. Click or tap Create Folder.

5. Type a name for the new folder.

6. Click or tap OK. The new folder is added to the list on the left side of the Mail app. Click OK to close the message box that tells you the folder has been created.

7. Tap or click Move in the Mail app options and a list of folders appears.

8. Tap the folder in which you want to save the message, and the Mail app files the message without any further action from you.

Marking Mail as Junk

It's just part of emailing today—you are going to get junk mail. To get rid of the junk mail you receive, select the message, swipe up from the bottom of the Mail window, and tap or click Move. When the folder list appears, tap or click Junk and the mail you selected moves to that folder.

Keeping Your Dates Straight with the Calendar App

Whether you're using your desktop PC or you're zooming around the countryside with your tablet, you need to know when your appointments are, who they're with, where you need to be, and when. The Calendar app can give you all that information, not only when you tap or click the app to open it on your screen, but anytime you glance at your Windows 8.1 computer. Because the Calendar app offers live notifications, you can have Windows display your appointments on the Lock screen of your computer, so you don't even have to log in to see what's next in your day.

Checking Today's Appointments

The first place you'll see your calendar information is on the Lock screen of your computer. You'll also notice the live tile updates on the Calendar app tile on the Start screen. You can tap the Calendar app to display your calendar, which opens by default in monthly view.

1. On the Start screen, tap or click the Calendar app. The first screen shows you any appointments you have coming up in the near future.

2. Swipe up from the bottom of the screen or right-click toward the bottom of the screen to display the apps bar.

3. Tap Day to switch the view to show the current day, as well as tomorrow.

4. Scroll down to review appointments later in the day.

5. Tap to review a specific appointment.

Adding a New Appointment

Creating a new appointment takes just a couple of taps or clicks and a little typing. You swipe up to display the apps bar and tap or click New, and then enter the information relevant to the appointment you're noting.

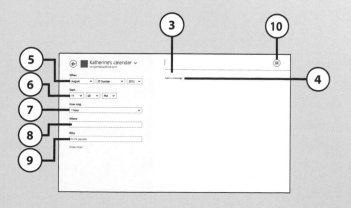

1. In the Calendar app, swipe up to display the apps bar.

2. Tap New. A blank appointment form opens so that you can enter information about the appointment.

3. Type a title for the appointment.

4. Enter a message describing the appointment.

5. Choose the date for the appointment.

6. Select the start time.

7. Choose the duration of the appointment.

8. Enter the location where it will be held.

9. Invite others to the event.

10. Tap or click Save.

Getting Specific with It

Click or tap Show More if you want to enter additional details about your appointment. For example, you can set the appointment to recur, choose when you want to receive reminders, and invite people to the event.

Making an Appointment Private

If you want to make sure that an appointment doesn't show up on a shared or public calendar, scroll down and click the Private check box at the bottom of the left panel in the new appointment screen after you've clicked Show More. You'll be able to see the appointment in your calendar, but others who have permission to view your calendar will not see it.

>>>Go Further

INVITING OTHERS TO YOUR SHINDIG

While you're filling in the details for your new appointment, you can invite others to participate. In the panel on the left side of the appointment window, tap or click in the Who box, and type the email addresses of the people you'd like to invite.

After you're finished filling out the appointment form, tap Send to send the invitation to everyone involved. Each person receives an invitation with Accept, Tentative, Decline, Propose New Time, and Respond at the top so that they can take immediate action in response to your invitation.

The Photos app in Windows
8.1 now includes a variety
of picture editing tools.

The Xbox Music app has been
redesigned and gives you access
to your collections, radio, or
unlimited albums and artists.

In this chapter, you learn how work with photos, music, video, and games by learning about these tasks:

→ Organizing and editing your photos

→ Your music, your way

→ Finding and watching your favorite shows

→ Playing games in Windows 8.1

Media and More

One of the big plans—or so we thought—with Windows 8 was to connect it easily to everything. In this day of media, we have photos, video clips, and music stored everywhere. We listen to podcasts on our phones, download pictures from our phones, and watch a video clip whenever we've got a few free moments and a video-capable device. The first release of Windows 8 made it easy to connect your various media apps to non-Microsoft programs and sites that are popular with end users—namely, Facebook and Flickr. For reasons that escape me, Windows 8.1 limits this type of shared access to the folders on This PC and, if you're lucky, your cloud storage.

This chapter focuses on the media features you'll find in Windows 8.1 as we go through these growing pains on the way to "connected everything."

Organizing and Editing Your Photos

If you're like me, you probably take photos of just about everything, now that cameras are part of our daily life (thanks to cellphone cameras). Taking photos is now a natural part of the way we communicate with friends, family, and colleagues. In addition to describing something to others—whether we do that in person, on the phone, or by email—now we can *show* them what we're talking about, using images we capture on our phones, tablets, or digital cameras.

Pictures are also a big part of the way we connect in social media as we share pictures with each other, tag friends and family members in group images, and post photos in places where others can view them. Although in Windows 8, developers allowed connectivity with other photo-sharing accounts—such as Facebook and Flickr—now with Windows 8.1, that interconnectivity has been taken away. Instead, Microsoft has added the ability to edit the photos you store locally, betting on the idea that our favorite photo-sharing sites will make apps available in the Windows Store that we can use to share our photos as we'd like. (I for one am hoping Microsoft rethinks this and adds account sharing back to the Photos app.)

Launching the Photos App

It's no surprise that the easiest way to launch the Photos app in Windows 8.1 is to tap or click the Photos app tile on the Start screen. When you launch the app, it opens and displays the folders in which your various photos are currently stored.

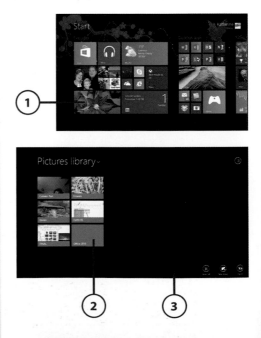

1. Tap or click the Photos app.

2. Tap a folder to display the photos contained inside it.

3. Swipe up or right-click the bottom of the screen to display the options bar and view additional photo choices.

Viewing Your Photos

The photos on your computer or device are available in your Photos app. You can choose the albums you want to view and scroll through your photos easily.

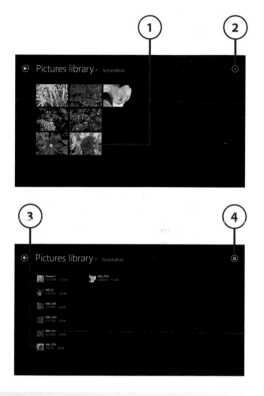

1. In the Photos app window, tap the folder containing the photos you want to view.

2. Change the way images are displayed, if you like tapping or clicking Details.

3. Tap or click the photo you want to view.

4. When you want to change the display back to Thumbnails view, tap or click Thumbnails.

Adding a Photo Folder

You can easily add folders—and folders within folders—to organize your photos in a way that makes sense to you. For example, you might have a Family folder and then create subfolders for family events within that folder. Or you might create a Projects folder and then create subfolders with individual names of projects so you can organize the photos in a way so that you can find them easily.

1. Display the Photos app.
2. Navigate to the folder where you want to add the folder.
3. Swipe up or right-click along the bottom of the screen.
4. Tap or click New Folder.

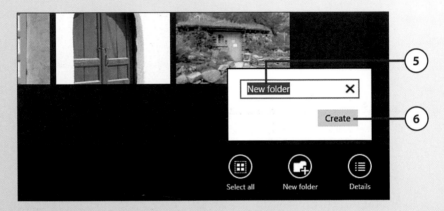

5. Type a name for the new folder.
6. Tap or click Create. The new folder is added to the current display.

Organizing Photos

After you create the new folders you need, they appear along the left side of the Photos app window. You can easily move photos into the new folders by cutting and pasting them from their current location into the new spot where you want them to be stored.

1. Display the folder containing the photos you want to organize.

2. Right-click or swipe down on each photo you want to move.

3. Click or tap Cut in the options bar.

4. Tap or click the folder where you want to store the photos.

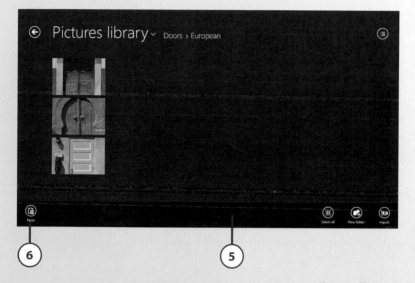

5. Swipe up or right-click the bottom of the screen to display the options bar.

6. Tap or click Paste. The Photos app adds the photos to the displayed folder.

It's Not All Good

IMAGE ISN'T EVERYTHING

Another part of the clunkiness of the Photos app in Windows 8.1 is the non-functioning Undo key. Now if you paste photos in the wrong folder by mistake, you can't undo the operation with a simple Ctrl+Z. Instead, you have to select the photos again, use Cut to remove them from their current location, select the correct folder, and use Paste to put them there. That's a lot of work for something a single shortcut key used to do for us.

Editing Photos

The new editing features in Windows 8.1 enable you to autocorrect your images by adjusting the color, brightness, and more in a single tap or click. You can also apply filters as you like—including one black and white filter—and use a number of basic fixes to correct simple photo problems.

1. Tap or click the image you want to edit so it appears full-screen.

2. Right-click or swipe up on the bottom of the screen to display the Photo options.

3. Click or tap Edit.

4. Tap or click a filter to apply it to the photo.

5. Choose the tool you want to use on the photo. Additional choices related to the tool you selected appear along the right side of the screen.

6. Tap the option you want to use with the selected tool.

7. Complete the editing task. In this case, the Crop tool is selected, and you can drag the selection handles to change the size of the cropped image.

8. Tap or click Apply to keep your changes.

9. When you're finished editing, swipe up or right-click the bottom of the screen.

10. If you want to create a copy of the original picture that saves your edits, tap or click Save a Copy.

11. If you want to update the original version of the picture with your changes, tap or click Update Original.

12. If you want to reverse your most recent edit, click or tap Undo.

13. To abandon all editing changes, click or tap Cancel. A confirmation box appears telling you all changes will be lost. To continue, click or tap Cancel Anyway.

Setting Photo Options

After you select a photo in the Windows 8.1 Photo app, photo options become available in the apps bar that enable you to work with the photo in various ways. You can set the photo as the Photo app tile so that it appears in the tile on your Windows Start screen, you can choose to use the photo as your Windows Lock screen, you can view the image in its online app, you can delete the photo, you can offer feedback about the photo (thumbs up or thumbs down), or you can display the photo as part of a slideshow.

1. When a photo you like is displayed on your screen, swipe up from the bottom of the screen or right-click to display the apps bar.

2. Click or tap Set As. A list of options appears.

3. Tap or click Photos Tile to make this photo the image shown on the Photos app tile on the Windows 8.1 Start screen.

4. Tap or click Lock Screen to use this image as your Lock screen photo.

Fickle App Images

If you love taking photos, you might have a new photo favorite every 15 minutes. You can change the photo used for your app tile on your Windows Start screen as often as you like—daily, hourly, or even more often, if you're so inclined. Just display your favorite photo in full-screen view, swipe up from the bottom of the screen (or double-click), tap or click Set As, and choose Photos Tile. You can change the photo options so the images displayed on the app tile are shuffled, which will continually display new images, like an app tile slide-show. With the Photos app open on the screen, swipe in from the right to display the Charms bar and tap or click Settings. Tap or click Options. Change the setting for Shuffle Photos on the Photos Tile from Off to On. When you return to the Start screen, the pictures on your app tile will refresh every few seconds.

Displaying a Slideshow

Windows 8.1 now enables you to display a slideshow not only in the Photos app, but also on your Lock screen. (To find out how to display a slideshow on your Lock screen, refer to Chapter 3, "Using and Tweaking the Start Screen.") You can display a slideshow of all the images in the current album while you're viewing your photos in the Photos app.

1. Display a picture in the folder you want to use for the slideshow.

2. Swipe up from the bottom or right-click to display the apps bar containing your photo options.

3. Tap or click Slide Show. The first photo in the album appears full-screen and after a few seconds, the next photo appears, and then the next. You can stop the slideshow by pressing Esc or by redisplaying the apps bar.

>>>Go Further

MANAGING YOUR SLIDESHOW IN THE PICTURE LIBRARY

You can also view and work with your photos using File Explorer, which you can access either from the Start screen (by clicking or tapping the File Explorer tile) or from the Windows desktop (by clicking or tapping the File Explorer icon in the Quick Launch bar).

Display the folder containing the photos you want to view and select one of the photos. Click the Picture Tools Manage tab and click Slide Show in the View group. The photos begin to appear on your screen.

You can control the speed and order of the display of the photos by right-clicking the screen. A context menu appears offering you the option of choosing Shuffle or Loop for the order of the photos. You can also select Slow, Medium, or Fast for the speed of the slideshow. Click outside the context menu to hide it and continue watching the show.

Ready, Set, Camera

Windows 8.1 also includes a Camera app that you can use to grab your own still photos or videos. You'll find the Camera app on the Start screen, and when you tap or click it, after asking whether the app can use your location, you'll see yourself—surprise!—on the screen, with two tools to the right, offering you the option of taking snapshots or choosing video. You can also swipe up from the bottom of the screen (or right-click) to display additional options that give you access to the Camera Roll, let you set an automated timer, or control the exposure of the photo or video you're grabbing with the camera.

Your Music, Your Way

In earlier versions of Windows, if you wanted to add some background music to your work—or put on some tunes for a party you were throwing—you had to go looking for Windows Media Player or Windows Media Center. In Windows 8.1, your media is front and center. You can get to your Music app right from the Start screen, with a simple tap or click. You can play your music in your own collection, search for the latest tunes from your favorite artists, and even purchase new music, all within the Music app.

In Windows 8.1, some of the changes to the Music app include a new design for the Music app interface, including easier access to your music collections and playlists, radio stations, and an unending catalog of tunes. The playback controls are located in the lower-right corner of the screen where you can always find them easily, too.

Getting Started with the Music App

The Music app is displayed as a tile on your Start screen, and you launch it by tapping or clicking the app tile. After you open the app, you'll see a screen similar to the Windows Store, where you can scroll through the various categories of songs and purchase and download new music.

1. On the Start screen, tap or click the Music app tile. The Music app opens on your screen.

2. Enter the name of an artist or album you want to search for.

3. Tap or click the button that reflects what you want to do.

4. Choose to create a new playlist.

5. Click or tap to import a playlist you've already created.

6. Change the volume for playback.

Playing Your Own Music

When you want to access the music you already have stored on your Windows PC or device, you can use the Music app to play the songs in your Music library. Your files appear by default in the Collections area, and Windows gives you the option of sharing your music with other devices as well.

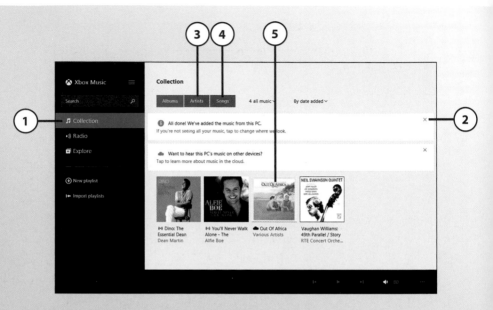

1. Tap or click Collection on the left side of the Music app screen.

2. Read any messages the app has for you and click Close to hide the message.

3. Tap or click to see your music sorted by artist.

4. Click or tap to display your music organized by song title.

5. Click or tap the album you want to play. The album page appears so that you can choose the song(s) you want to listen to.

6. Click or tap the song you'd like to play.

7. Tap or click + to display an options list so that you can add the song to the Now Playing playlist or create a new playlist that includes that song.

8. Tap or click Play to begin playing the song without adding it to a playlist.

9. Tap or click to play the entire album.

10. Display information about the album.

11. Return to the Music app while you listen to the song so you can continue browsing.

Finding Your Music in the Cloud

You can let the Music app know where to find your music by selecting the location in the Collection screen. At the top of the screen, click or tap the Music arrow to the right of the Albums, Artists, and Songs buttons (refer to Figure 11.18). A small options list appears, offering you three choices: All Music, On This PC, and In the Cloud. To tell the Music app to find your music in the cloud, choose In The Cloud (no big surprise there).

Finding Music You Like

The Music app is organized so you can browse through songs in the genres you like most, or you can use the Search charm to locate songs by a particular artist you're partial to.

1. In the Music app window, tap Explore. A revolving list of artists appears on the right side of the screen. If you scroll down, you'll see New Albums and Top Albums categories.

2. Tap or click View All. A screen appears showing you a collection of new albums.

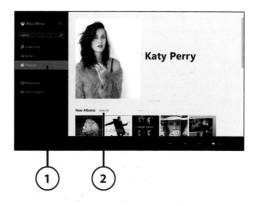

3. Click or tap the All Genres arrow.

4. Scroll through the list to find the genre you'd like to hear. Tap the genre selection.

5. Tap or click the album you want to listen to.

6. Click or tap the song you'd like to listen to.

7. Add to a playlist.

8. Play the song.

9. Return to the albums list.

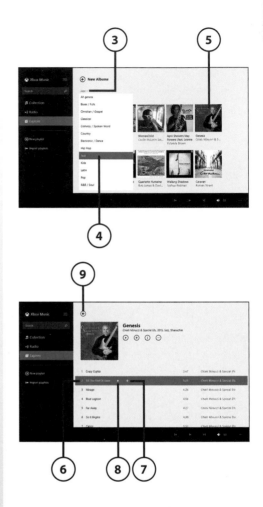

Creating a Radio Station

If you like to listen to a specific type of music, or a favorite artist, but like to mix up the tunes while you listen, you can create your own radio station.

1. Click or tap Radio to display the Radio screen.

2. Tap or click Start a Station.

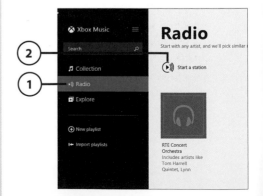

3. Enter the name of an artist or group you want to listen to.

4. Click or tap the radio listing you'd like to hear. The Xbox Music app chooses music related to the artist you selected and starts playing the first song automatically.

5. Use the playback controls to move among songs in the radio station.

Finding and Watching Your Favorite Shows

It can be tempting to watch videos and browse TV shows while you're supposed to be working on the sales presentation you need to give at next week's meeting. You'll have to discipline yourself—to a point. The Video app in Windows is tempting, giving you access to streaming movies, television shows, and the videos you add to your own collection after purchasing them in the marketplace. You can find out more about your favorite movies and shows and even rent them online instantly and then stream them to your computer or to your Xbox.

WHERE'S MEDIA CENTER?

Microsoft removed Windows Media Center from Windows 8, much to the dismay of Media Center users who use the utility to record and view televisions shows and movies. Microsoft opted to include Windows Media Center only in Windows 8 Professional, although it is also available as a separate download, which users can purchase as an upgrade.

Windows Media Player is still a part of Windows 8, but without the ability to play DVDs. I guess we'll have to use our Xboxes to do that. Maybe that's part of the grand plan.

Exploring Video

Similar to the Photos app and the Music app, you launch the Video app by tapping or clicking the Video tile on the Start screen. Unlike the Music app, which got a big redesign in Windows 8.1, the Video app screen resembles the configuration users saw in the first release of Windows 8. The Home area spotlights a selection of shows, and recommendations suggest videos Xbox Video thinks you may like. You can swipe or scroll to the right to see New Movies, Featured Movies, New TV Shows, Featured TV Shows. And if you scroll to the left from Home, you'll see your Personal Videos and My TV, which displays videos and shows you've previously purchased. You can locate, preview, and buy or rent the movies and shows you want to watch.

1. Tap or click the Video app tile on the Windows Start screen, and the Video app preview appears.

2. Scroll to the right to display the additional categories.

3. Tap a category to preview the movies or TV shows within it.

4. Tap the tile of any selection you'd like to know more about.

5. Tap or click to play the movie trailer.

6. Tap or click to buy or rent the video.

Is This an Overnight Rental?

When you rent a movie from the Movies Store, you have 14 days—or 24 hours from the time you start watching the movie—in which to view it. Since it costs $4.99 to purchase 400 Microsoft points, and current movies often cost 480 points, you may not be getting such a deal—but it is convenient to just tap a button on your Windows PC and watch an Academy award-winning movie soon after it has left the theatre.

>>>Go Further

USING XBOX SMARTGLASS

Xbox SmartGlass is an app that enables you to connect your Windows 8.1 computer to your Xbox 360 and stream music and video to your heart's content. If you have an Xbox and want to connect it to the media you're using in Windows 8.1, you will be prompted automatically to download the Xbox SmartGlass when you tap or click Play on Xbox. You can tap or click the Get Xbox SmartGlass from the Store link to go directly to the Windows Store.

Xbox SmartGlass is a free utility; simply tap or click Install to install it on your computer. The app will appear on the far-right side of your Start screen.

When you tap the Xbox SmartGlass tile, a screen appears giving you the instructions for connecting your Xbox to your PC. Simply log in to your account on your Xbox, and navigate to System Settings, choose Console Settings, and select Xbox SmartGlass. Then choose Available.

Return to your PC and tap Connect when prompted, and your PC and your Xbox will talk to each other and synchronize your media. This makes it super simple for you to find a movie, for example, and with a few easy taps, stream the movie live to your family room for everyone to enjoy.

Don't Forget Your Favorite Shows

You can use the Xbox Video app to find and stream your favorite TV episodes on your computer or your Xbox as well. When you scroll to the right and tap or click on the TV categories, you can choose to display shows sorted into two categories: new TV shows, or featured TV shows.

1. In the Xbox Video app, tap or click the cover image of the series you want to view. Choose View Seasons to display the specific episodes in the season available in the TV Store.

2. If you want to buy the whole season, tap or click Buy Season.

3. If you want to buy only a single episode, review your episode choices and tap the one you want to view.

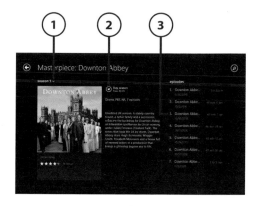

4. Tap or click Buy Episode to view the episode. The Confirm Purchase screen appears so that you can click Confirm to use your Microsoft Points to buy the show. It will then become available in your collection so that you can watch the show when you wish.

Confirming Your Purchase

You might need to enter your password to confirm your identity before you can purchase a movie or TV show in the Xbox Video app. The process can be a bit tedious, but it's better to be safe than sorry, and you want Microsoft to be careful with your online purchases.

Playing Games with Windows 8.1

You can use the Games app to play your favorite games, see what's hot in the world of gaming, and buy new games you'd like to try. Depending on the format of the game, you might be able to play it on your PC or the Xbox, or both. Begin by displaying the Games app by tapping the app tile on your Start screen.

Finding and Playing Your Favorite Games

The Game Activity area of the Games app displays all the games you have purchased and played on your Xbox, Xbox Kinect, or Xbox Live accounts. You can display more information about the games or—in some cases—play the game on your PC by tapping the one you want to see.

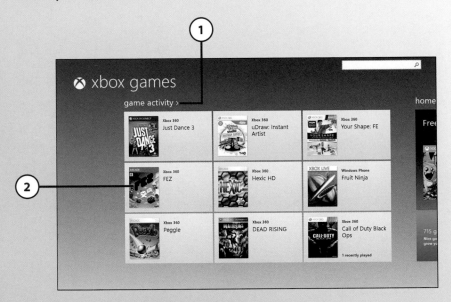

1. Scroll to the Game Activity area of the Xbox Games screen.

2. Tap or click the tile of a game you want to play.

Can I Play This on My PC?

The games you can play on your computer have an Xbox Live banner at the top of the game cover. For games that can only be played on your Xbox system, you'll see either Xbox 360 Kinect or Xbox 360 at the top of the game image.

Buying a Game

You can find games to purchase or rent in the Windows Games Store. You can display the Windows Games Store by swiping to the right and tapping the Windows Games Store category.

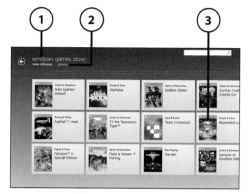

1. Display the Windows Games Store.

2. By default, new releases are shown, but if you want to see games listed by category, tap or click Genres.

3. Tap or click a game tile to display more about the game.

4. Tap or click Play to begin playing the game. If you don't own the game, when you choose Play the next screen will give you the option of buying the game or trying it.

5. Tap or click Explore Game to read more about the game, show the leaderboards, see what other users have achieved in the game, and more.

SENDING OUT A BEACON FOR YOU

You can also set a beacon to let your friends know that you're interested in playing a specific game online. Your friends and contacts in your social network and on Xbox LIVE will know that you want to play *Fable III*, for example, and they can respond by inviting you to play a game.

To set your beacon for a specific game, display the game and choose Explore Game. In the screen that appears, tap or click Set Beacon in the game description area. A text box opens with the text "I want to play this game with friends," and you can tap or click Set to set the beacon. If you change your mind, you can click Cancel instead.

SkyDrive makes it easy for
you to store, share, and
update files in the cloud.

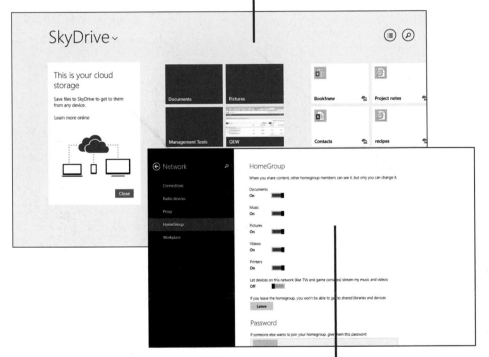

With a HomeGroup, you can
share files of all types among
all the computers in your home.

In this chapter, you learn to work with your files in the cloud by mastering these tasks:

→ Working with SkyDrive
→ Getting started with a HomeGroup
→ Using your HomeGroup

Working in the Cloud

Keeping you connected is one of the major goals of Windows 8.1, and now having the capability to store and retrieve files from the cloud is an important part of your operating system. This means you can easily save files and folders to the cloud, where you can access them using your phone, tablet, or computers at various locations. That can be a real time-saver and also help you ensure you're not duplicating your efforts—or creating copies of files you'll never use—by syncing everything with your free storage online.

What's in a Name?

SkyDrive is Microsoft's in-the-cloud offering, but in the not-too-distant future, Microsoft will be giving SkyDrive a new name. So although that's the name in use as we're preparing this book for you, at some point, expect a change. (Hopefully, new name or not, all the tasks and techniques we offer here will work without a hitch.)

You also might want to connect with your home network or create a HomeGroup, which enables you to easily share files, pictures, music, and more among the various computers in your home. The future is now! And enjoying it feels easier than ever.

Working with SkyDrive

SkyDrive is Microsoft's in-the-cloud app that makes it simple for you to save and access files in the cloud as easily as you can use files on your own computer. If you want to save files sporadically as you work—perhaps you created a great document design you want to save somewhere safe—you can save them to your space in the cloud, where you can access them from any computer or device that has web access. The SkyDrive app on your Start screen gives you easy access to your SkyDrive files, and you can navigate to the folder you want and store additional files there as often as you'd like.

Launching SkyDrive

You'll find SkyDrive on your Start screen, and you can launch it with a tap or click.

1. Click or tap the SkyDrive app tile on your Start screen.

Accessing Files in the Cloud

The first time you launch the SkyDrive app, Windows 8.1 displays some help information along the left side of the screen. You can click the Learn More link to go to a site online where Microsoft will be glad to give you a basic introduction to SkyDrive. If you'd rather jump in and start exploring, you can tap a folder and learn how to store your files.

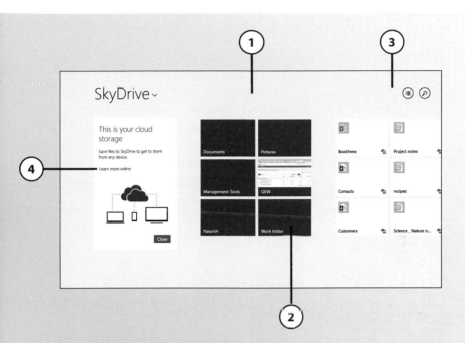

1. Launch SkyDrive and the initial SkyDrive screen appears.

2. Tap or click a folder to open it.

3. SkyDrive lets you know about any items that are synching. Click or tap the link to see the progress of the download.

4. Click or tap to learn more about SkyDrive.

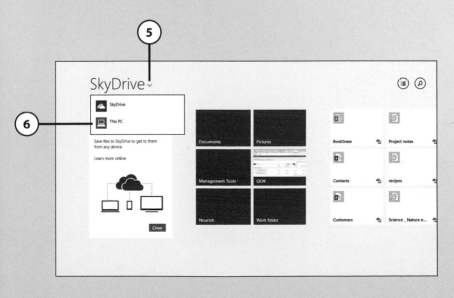

5. Choose a different location, if you like, by clicking the SkyDrive arrow.

6. Click or tap the location where you want to access files.

Saving Files to SkyDrive

Your Windows 8.1 apps will enable you to store files to SkyDrive by default. In fact, when you work in File Explorer, you'll see SkyDrive in the Favorites area on the upper-left side of the File Explorer window. You can easily add files to your SkyDrive folder and let the app sync the files automatically for you. If you want to work in the cloud, however, you can also add the files you choose easily, using the method described here.

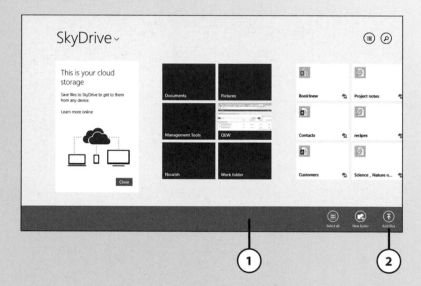

1. Swipe up from the bottom or right-click toward the bottom of the screen to display SkyDrive options.

2. Tap or click Add Items.

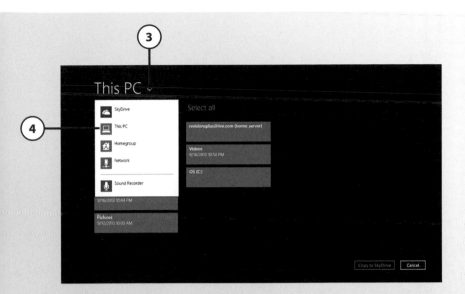

3. Click the This PC arrow to display the places where your files are stored.

4. Click or tap the place with the files you want to add to SkyDrive (for example, This PC).

5. Tap a folder to display additional files if necessary.

6. Swipe down or right-click individual files you want to add to SkyDrive. SkyDrive displays the selected files at the bottom of the screen.

7. Tap or click Copy to SkyDrive. The files are uploaded to the SkyDrive folder you selected. SkyDrive gives you the status of the copy process by displaying a message in the upper-right corner of your screen.

WHAT ABOUT FILES I DON'T WANT IN THE CLOUD?

As your storage in the cloud, SkyDrive is a bit different from a drive connected to your computer. Instead of a storage area, where you can place files and then download some but not others, SkyDrive serves as storage that is automatically synced with the cloud for you. This means there's no way to exclude a file from this synchronization process; everything in your SkyDrive folder is synced automatically with the cloud. If you want to keep a file on your local computer but not sync it to the cloud, keep it stored on This PC and don't put it in your SkyDrive folder.

Managing Files in SkyDrive

After you add files to SkyDrive, chances are you'll want to move them around, copy or rename them, or open them with the app of your choosing. You can do all this right from the SkyDrive screen.

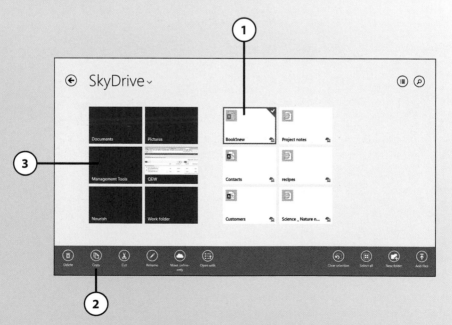

1. Tap or click the file (or files) you want to manage. The options bar appears.

2. Click the tool you want to use. For example, tap or click Copy.

3. Choose the folder where you want to put the file.

4. Swipe up or right-click the screen. The options bar appears.

5. Tap or click Paste, and SkyDrive pastes the file in the new location.

Make That File Online Only

By default, SkyDrive makes the files you place in the cloud also available to you when you're offline by maintaining a synchronized copy on This PC. If you want a file to be stored in the cloud only, display the folder containing the file and swipe up or right-click the screen. In the options bar, choose Make Online-Only, and SkyDrive will no longer make the file available when you're offline.

SOLVING SYNC PROBLEMS

Occasionally SkyDrive might have trouble with one file or another. When the app has trouble syncing a file, the folder containing the file will give you a message: Needs Attention. When you tap or click the Needs Attention link, it may lead you into a subfolder and finally to a file where the upload has failed or there has been another problem getting the file into the cloud.

The nice thing about this is that SkyDrive leads you directly to the source of the problem, where an error message then gives you an indication of what to do. For example, in Word, you might see an error message like this:

UPLOAD FAILED We're sorry, someone updated the server copy and it's not possible to upload your changes now.

In this case, Word gives two options: Keep My Version or Keep Server Version. When you click your choice, Word displays a message box letting you know what the outcome of that action will be. When you confirm the action, the file is synced and the sync problem is resolved.

Getting Started with a HomeGroup

A HomeGroup gives you a simple way to share music, media, and other libraries on your PC with other computers in your home. This means someone using the living room PC can watch a video clip that is on your computer in your office upstairs; your Xbox 360 can play music and slideshows from another computer; and you can share printers and other resources that you set up as part of your HomeGroup.

Setting up a HomeGroup is a simple task. A HomeGroup category in PC Settings enables you to join a HomeGroup and adjust HomeGroup settings for the computers and devices participating. You can let Windows know whether you want to share documents, music, pictures, videos, and printers and other devices on the network.

Setting Up a HomeGroup

By default, Windows 8.1 sets up a new HomeGroup automatically for your home network or, if you already have an existing HomeGroup on your home network (suppose, for example, that you have a Windows 7 desktop PC on which Windows 7 already created a HomeGroup), Windows 8.1 will ask whether you want to join the existing HomeGroup. You can then go to the other computers in your home and add them (which is covered in the next section, "Joining a HomeGroup"). To view the HomeGroup that Windows has already set up, follow these steps:

1. Display the Charms bar and tap or click Settings; then choose Change PC Settings.

2. In PC Settings, scroll down and click or tap Network, and then tap HomeGroup.

3. If you are already part of a HomeGroup, the settings for your various files will appear. Review the current settings for your file types and devices.

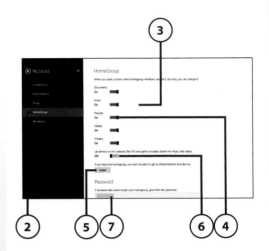

4. To turn on sharing for a particular item, drag the slider from the left to the right. To turn off sharing, drag the slider from the right to the left.

5. If you want to remove your computer from the HomeGroup, tap or click Leave.

6. Turn on sharing if you want TVs and game consoles, like the Xbox 360, to be able to access the content on your computer.

7. If you plan to set up other computers in your home so they can access this HomeGroup, write down the Membership password to enter on the other computers when prompted.

New Files in Shared Libraries

When you indicate the libraries you want to share, this means that all files—present and future—that are part of those libraries will be shared. You will be able to view and change the files you share, and others will be able only to view, but not change, the files. So if you add files to the libraries later, others in your HomeGroup will also be able to view those new files.

Joining a HomeGroup

After you set up the HomeGroup that has been created on your home network, you can easily add other computers to the group. You need the password you noted in the preceding section as you set up the other computers on the HomeGroup. Use the following steps to add the other computers to your HomeGroup:

1. Display the HomeGroup page in the Network screen of PC Settings.

2. Enter the password you've been given for the HomeGroup you want to join.

3. Click Join. Windows 8.1 connects you to the existing HomeGroup and displays the various shared settings in the top of the HomeGroup screen.

Synchronize Your Watches

Because all computers in a HomeGroup must have synchronized clocks, make sure that all your computers are set to use Internet time so you can be confident the time is accurate. You can set the time to Internet time by going to Date and Time Settings on your computer and making sure the Set Time Automatically setting is turned On in the Date and Time screen.

Using Your HomeGroup

Each computer in your HomeGroup has its own set of shared settings. For example, you might share only Documents and Music on your computer, but someone else in your house might want to share all content types. The actual content you can access depends on what each user chooses to share when setting up or joining the workgroup. If one user decides not to share her music, for example, the other computers in the HomeGroup aren't able to access the music on that particular PC.

Viewing Your HomeGroup

You can easily access the various computers in your HomeGroup by using File Explorer. The HomeGroup appears in the navigation pane on the left side of the screen, just above This PC.

1. Display the Desktop.

2. Tap or click the File Explorer icon in the Quick Launch area of the Desktop taskbar. File Explorer launches.

3. Click or tap HomeGroup in the left pane. The computers in your HomeGroup appear in the Details pane.

Visible HomeGroup Computers

Note that the HomeGroup computers you can see when you're viewing the HomeGroup in File Explorer do not include the one you're using. Instead, File Explorer shows you the other HomeGroup computers on your network. This enables you to view and choose files on those computers through the HomeGroup while still accessing the files on your own computer using the traditional route— clicking your own Documents, Music, Pictures, or Videos folders.

Accessing Files on Shared Computers

After you know where to find the other computers on your HomeGroup, you can easily access the files and folders that have been shared with you. Here's how:

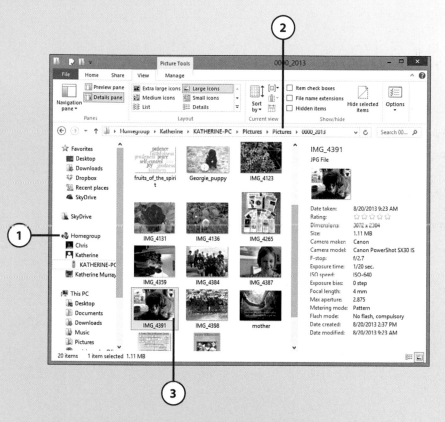

1. In File Explorer, click or tap HomeGroup in the left pane.

2. Click the folder you want to view.

3. In the center column, click the file you want to view or play. Click the tool in the ribbon at the top of the File Explorer window that matches the action you'd like to take.

Changing Your Mind About Sharing

If you decide after the fact that you would rather not share some of the libraries you've shared with your HomeGroup, you can turn off sharing of those
folders. On the Start screen, type **homegroup** and tap or click Settings. Tap or
click Choose HomeGroup and Sharing Options. When the HomeGroup page
of the Network settings appears, you can change the sharing settings for your
Documents, Music, Pictures, and Videos folders, as well as the sharing settings
for your Printers and Devices. Additionally, you can change the sharing settings
for your media devices, such as game consoles and TVs. Close the PC Settings
window after you make your changes and Windows saves them automatically.

SHARING A PRINTER ON THE HOMEGROUP

>>>Go Further

If you have a wireless printer that connects to your router, you can print
from any computer in your HomeGroup. If you are using a traditional
printer connected to one of the computers by a printer cable, all is
not lost.

You can still log in to the computer to which the printer is attached, access
the document using the HomeGroup shared files, and print from the computer with printer access. Nice.

Choose automatic
updates so you always
have the most recent
release of Windows.

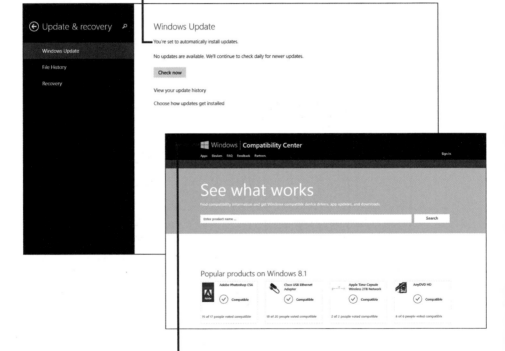

You can easily make
sure your software and
devices are compatible
with Windows.

In this chapter, you learn how to care for your PC and solve problems when they arise by learning about these tasks:

→ Getting Windows updates

→ Backing up and restoring your files

→ Optimizing your computer

→ Checking Windows compatibility

Feeding and Troubleshooting Your PC

Your computer—whether it's a desktop PC, a tablet, or a netbook—needs consistent care to stay healthy. In today's virus-ripe landscape, keeping your computer healthy means making sure your Windows updates are current, you run antivirus programs regularly, and your files are organized in such a way that they are making the best use of your hard disk space. This chapter introduces you to ways you can ensure that your software is up-to-date and shows you System Tools that will help you keep everything in order.

Getting Windows Updates

One of the most important things you can do for your PC is make sure you're signed up to receive automatic updates. Updates can provide new security features, bug fixes, and more, so they are important for keeping your computer as up-to-date as possible. You can let Windows know how to check for and install any available program updates, choosing, if you prefer, for the computer to do it at some point when you're not using it. When you let your computer update automatically, it downloads any new updates and installs them at the time you specified.

Turning On Automatic Updates

First you need to tell Windows 8.1 how you want to check for updates and install them as needed. You can have Windows do it all automatically. You can also choose to have Windows let you know when updates are available so you can download and install them when you're ready.

1. Display the Charms and tap Settings; choose Change PC Settings.

2. In the PC Settings screen, click or tap Update and Recovery.

3. Tap or click Choose How Updates Get Installed.

4. Tap or click the Important Updates arrow and tap or click the setting of your choice. Install Updates Automatically is selected by default; this causes Windows to download and install all updates without any action from you. Your other choices are Download Updates But Let Me Choose Whether to Install Them, Check for Updates But Let Me Choose Whether to Download and Install Them, and Never Check for Updates.

5. Click to clear the Recommended Updates check box if you want to limit the updates you receive to only those that are considered important for the functioning of the software or your PC security.

6. Click to clear the Give Me Updates for Microsoft Products check box if you don't want to receive updates for other Microsoft products and check for new software when your updates are downloaded.

7. Click Apply to save your changes.

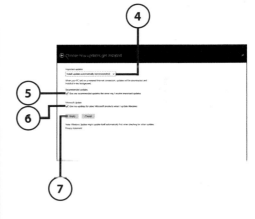

Best-Practice Updating

Microsoft recommends that you set your update schedule so that you're receiving updates at least once every week. When important updates are released, they typically arrive on the second or fourth Tuesday of the month. There are intermittent releases, however, so checking more frequently than every two weeks is a good idea.

Choosing a Time for Automatic Updates

The best time to schedule your program updates, of course, is the time you're not using your computer. Windows enables you to choose the time you want the updates to be downloaded and installed. What's more, you can give Windows 8.1 permission to wake up your computer at the time you specify.

1. On the Windows Start screen, start to type **automatic maintenance**.

2. This time, tap or click Change Automatic Maintenance Settings.

3. In the Automatic Maintenance dialog box, click the arrow to the right of Run Maintenance Tasks Daily at, and click the time when you want to schedule the updates.

4. Click the Allow Scheduled Maintenance to Wake Up My Computer check box if you want the updates to be done whether your computer is awake or not.

5. Click OK to save your changes.

The Wake-able Computer

When you tell Windows that you want it to wake up your computer to check for and install updates, be sure to leave the computer in sleep mode as opposed to turning off the power. If you turn off your computer, Windows won't be able to access the computer to do the automatic updates.

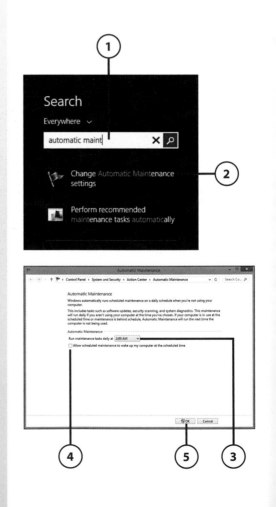

Checking for Updates Manually

You can check manually for updates instead of relying solely on the automatic updating system. You might do this, for example, when you have heard that a new update is available for a specific feature or you have been waiting for a coming upgrade that will impact Windows features you care about.

1. On the Start screen, type **windows update**.

2. Tap or click Windows Update. The Windows Update dialog box appears.

3. Tap or click Check for Updates. The right panel shows you the current setting of your automatic updates and lets you know the last time updates were checked. Windows checks for updates and lists any found updates in the Windows Update area, where you can review and install them if you want.

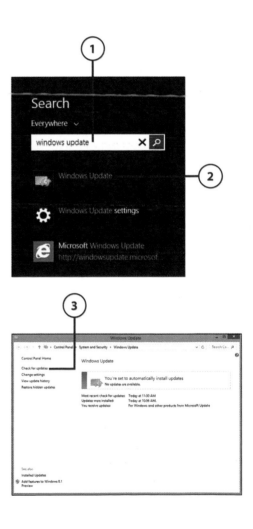

REVIEWING UPDATE HISTORY

If you're wondering what kinds of updates Windows has already performed without your knowledge, you can check out the update history to see the full list. In the Windows Update window, click View Update History. A large list of updates appears, and you can get more information about individual updates that were performed by double-clicking the update name.

When you finish reviewing updates, click OK to close the Review Your Update History window.

Backing Up and Restoring Your Files

You might already be making copies of important files and tucking them away someplace safe—like copying them to an external hard disk, burning them to DVD, or saving them on a flash drive. If not, you should be. Making regular backups of your files helps you feel secure knowing that your files are protected and that you have an extra copy, just in case something happens. You can make these simple file backups yourself by using File Explorer to copy the files to the folder or device where you want to store the backup files.

Windows also provides a backup utility you can use to back up everything on your hard disk. You should do this larger backup regularly—perhaps once every month or so. This ensures that your files have been saved so that if something unexpected happens to your computer—for example, you wind up with a virus that damages important files—you can restore the files from your backup and go on as usual.

Another new feature built right in to Windows enables you to save your files directly to the cloud, where you don't have to worry about viruses or hard disk failure. In fact, Office 2013 applications—Word, Excel, PowerPoint, OneNote, Publisher, and Access—all save your files by default to your SkyDrive account (although you can change that default so the files are in fact saved on your computer if you choose).

Backing Up Your Files

The first step in backing up your files involves setting up the backup utility. When you do this, you tell Windows where you want to save the backup files and when you want to do the backup. You can change those settings at any time, of course, but Windows will take care of the backup for you automatically from here on out on the day and time you specify.

1. On the Start screen, type **backup**.

2. Tap or click Save Backup Copies of Your Files with File History. File History will want to back up your files to either an external hard drive or a network location.

3. In the File History dialog box, the utility lists where your files will be stored. Click the destination you want to use, and click Turn On. File History begins copying the files to the backup location you specified.

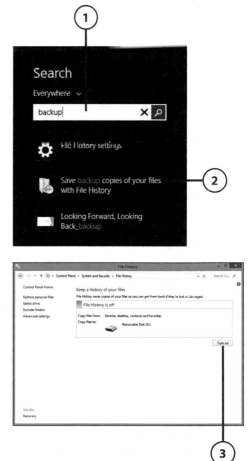

Choosing What to Back Up

You can tell Windows 8.1 how often you want to save files, how much space you want to devote to the backup files, and how long you want to keep file versions by clicking or tapping Advanced Settings on the left side of the File History dialog box. You can choose to save files as often as every 10 minutes or as infrequently as once a day. You can choose to allot anywhere from 2 percent to 20 percent of available disk space for your backups. And you can choose to keep files forever (which is the default) or choose from 1 month to 2 years—or until the space is needed, whichever comes first.

Restoring Files

You might not ever need the files you backed up—but it's good to have them just in case. Perhaps you accidentally deleted an important folder. Or maybe you had a computer problem and had to clean off your files and now you're ready to put the files back. Whatever the situation, Windows can easily restore your backed-up files.

1. On the Start screen, type **restore your files**.

2. Tap or click Restore Your Files with File History.

3. Click or tap the folder you want to restore.

4. Click the Restore to Original Location button.

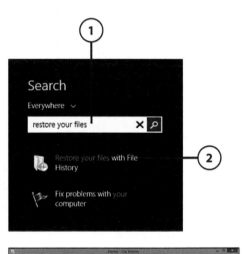

Merging or Skipping Folders

If you have an existing folder with the same name as the folder you're restoring, Windows will ask you whether you want to merge the folder with the existing one or skip it. Click your choice, and the files are restored.

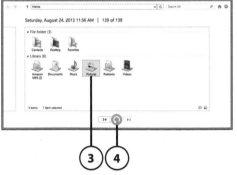

Optimizing Your Computer

Windows makes it easy for you to ensure that your computer is running as efficiently as possible.

As part of the normal wear and tear on a computer, file bits get scattered around the hard drive. Sure, when you look at the folders in File Explorer, everything looks nice and neat, but the way your computer is actually storing the data isn't quite that linear. Your computer knows where everything is, thanks to the way it indexes information, but over time, bits and pieces of files can be saved in various places all over the drive. And to present the file to you as a complete whole so you can work with it as usual, your computer has to do some behind-the-scenes processing. You can use the settings in the Optimize Drives dialog box to clean up your hard drive by consolidating those bits of files and putting them back together in one place again. This can help your computer process faster and better, which is a good thing.

Optimizing Your Hard Disk

Although it runs automatically by default, running the Optimize utility fairly regularly—such as once every month or two—will help you ensure that you're making the most of the available storage space on your hard drive.

1. On the Start screen, type **optimize**.

2. Tap or click Defragment and Optimize Your Drives.

3. In the Optimize Drives dialog box, click Analyze to do a check on the selected drive to see whether optimizing it will save you any space.

4. Click Optimize to defragment the selected disk.

5. After the process is finished, click Close.

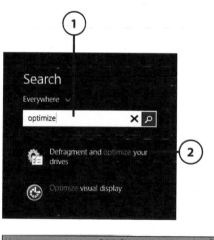

>>>Go Further

SCHEDULING REGULAR DEFRAGMENTING

You can put your PC on a steady defrag diet by having the system automatically defragment your hard drive at a specific time of the week or month. Click Change Settings in the Optimize Drives dialog box. In the Optimize Drives: Optimization Schedule dialog box, click the Run on a Schedule check box and click the Frequency you want: Daily, Weekly, or Monthly.

You can also click or tap the Choose button to select the drives you want to optimize following this schedule. Click OK to save your settings, and Disk Defragmenter will run automatically as you specified to keep your files as compact as possible.

Checking Windows Compatibility

Sure, you have a Windows 8.1 PC, but chances are you need to trade files and perhaps work with programs that were created long before Windows 8.1 came on the scene. A number of users face challenges in using software and hardware that weren't made to work with Windows 8.1. How can you get the programs and hardware working together to complete the tasks you need to get done? This section offers some resources that can help you resolve compatibility issues.

Using the Windows Compatibility Center

Microsoft recognizes that helping users know how to use their computers and programs together—no matter which Windows version they might be using—is an important part of supporting its product. For that reason, Microsoft has created the Windows Compatibility Center, which offers a wide range of software and hardware you can check for compatibility with Windows 8.1.

1. Launch IE 11 and type **windows compatibility center** in the address bar. As you type, Bing suggests links that offer the page you need.

2. In the search results that appear, click the link Windows Compatibility Center.

3. Alternately, you can click Go.

4. Type the program or hardware device you want to find on the site.

5. Click a popular category to search for compatible software.

6. Find devices that work with Windows 8.1. You can then review the list of products displayed to find the ones that are compatible with Windows 8.1. To learn more about a specific product, tap or click it; more information about the product and its compatibility appears in the browser window.

WORKING WITH WINDOWS TROUBLESHOOTERS

Windows includes a number of troubleshooters you can use to resolve issues you might be having with your PC or software. You can display all the various troubleshooters by typing **troubleshooting** on the Start screen and tapping or clicking Troubleshooting in the results list. You'll see a variety of troubleshooters, ranging from tools that help you sleuth out problems with files to tools for solving memory or network problems.

If none of the troubleshooters do the trick, type **help** and tap or click the Help and Support tab to browse for the help you need or contact Windows support.

The Windows Store has been
redesigned in Windows 8.1.

You can work with your apps
easily using the Store app.

This appendix introduces you to your apps and shows you around the Windows Store by exploring these topics:

→ Exploring your apps
→ Checking out the Bing apps
→ The Windows Store revisited

Windows 8.1 App Gallery

Apps were a big story in Windows 8, and the trend continues in Windows 8.1. They bring information from beyond your computer right to your Start screen. They offer fun and interesting information, beautiful pictures, weather forecasts, shopping, and much more—all in neat little packages that are pleasant to see and easy to use.

And—even better—many of the apps in the Windows Store are free, too. You can browse and search for specific apps and find all sorts of information online before you download and install what you find. A growing and vibrant user community is springing up in the Windows Store as well; use the reviews others have posted to help you decide which apps you want to install and then come back and post your own reviews so others benefit from your experience!

This appendix offers some of the common tasks you're likely to want to accomplish when you're finding, installing, and reviewing apps.

Exploring Your Apps

As you learned in Chapter 7, "Diving In with Apps," finding, arranging, launching, and closing apps in Windows is a simple task. They all work in a similar fashion—you just tap or click them to start the app—and they all display their app options when you swipe up from the bottom of your Windows screen.

Although that chapter showed you how to find and work with apps, we didn't take a detailed look at all the apps made available on your Start screen. As a quick review, here's a table of all the apps you'll find in Windows 8, along with a brief description of each one. In the section that follows, you learn more about the Bing apps that are part of Windows as well.

Introducing Your Windows 8 Apps

App Tile	App Name	Use This App To
	Windows Store	Browse, search, buy, and download new Windows apps
	People	Keep up to date with friends and family on social media
	Desktop	Display your Windows desktop to work with files and more
	Internet Explorer	Use IE 11 to browse the Web
	Mail	Check your email, send new messages, and organize messages you've received

App Tile	App Name	Use This App To
Linda's birthday All day Saturday 21	Calendar	Set appointments and review your calendar for the day, week, or month
Various Artists Mozart: Concerto For Cla... Xbox Music Music	Xbox Music	Find, preview, and purchase music or listen to your existing tunes
Video	Xbox Video	Search for and purchase new videos or clips on your PC or device
Photos	Photos	Organize, view, and download photos from all your photo accounts
UN: one-third of Syria's population displaced by war	News	Review today's top stories with compelling photos
Games	Xbox Games	Find and play your favorite Xbox LIVE games
61° Lawrence Partly Cloudy 85°/55° Weather	Bing Weather	Check the weather in your area or in other locations you specify
Camera	Camera	Take a snapshot or video using the webcam on your computer
Maps	Maps	Map your route to new destinations near and far

App Tile	App Name	Use This App To
	Bing Finance	Get the latest financial news and follow your favorite stocks
	Bing Travel	Learn about travel destinations and read articles about favorite spots
	Bing Sports	Get up-to-date sports headlines, scores, and more
	SkyDrive	Access the files stored in your own SkyDrive in the cloud

Checking Out the Bing Apps

The "Bing apps" are so called because they bring to your Windows Start screen specific information related to a particular topic, using the powerful search capabilities of Bing, Microsoft's popular search engine. The Bing apps you'll find on your desktop include Finance, Weather, Maps, News, Sports, and Travel.

Bing apps are available in 12 languages and can be used in 62 countries, which is pretty amazing given the newness of the whole app phenomenon. Bing apps of course are designed for touch interfaces but work great with a click of the mouse as well, and you can personalize and even aggregate (in some apps) the information you want to receive so you're always getting just what you want on your Start screen.

Finance App

If you're following the stock market and like to keep an eye on what's happening, you can use the Finance app to get an up-to-the-minute look at market conditions. The updating tile displays various indices, and you can easily check your favorite stocks and check all kinds of rates with a single touch or click.

The first screen you see when you launch the Finance app is the Bing Finance Today page, which offers the top financial news story as well as the current standing of the major indices. You can tap the headline to read the news story; tap the information icon to read the photo caption; or swipe to the left to display additional information, financial news, your own personal stock watchlist, and information about the big movers in the market. You can also set up the Finance app to display the information you want. Just click the links on the right side of the screen to get started.

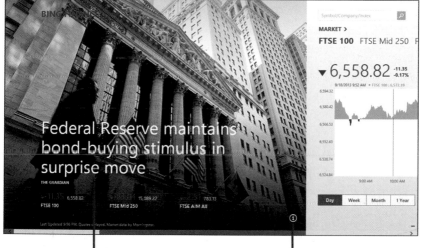

Tap or click title to read article　　　**Click or tap to read caption**

Weather App

The Weather app can make you feel better about the weather forecast, whether it's going to be rainy and cold or steamy and dry today, simply because the app itself is so beautiful. The Weather app uses your location information to find the weather in your local area and displays current conditions on your updating app tile on the Start screen. When you tap or click the tile, you see a five-day forecast. You can click the arrow to display an additional five days if you like or click the arrow to display additional information like Wind, Visibility, Humidity, and Barometer, as well as forecasts from other weather services.

Swiping left displays your hour-by-hour forecast, as well as a variety of maps showing regional temperatures, Doppler radar, local precipitation, and satellite maps. Continue scrolling right, and you'll get a historical account of today's weather, including highs and lows for the month, record highs and lows in history, and the weather stats (rainfall, snow days, and rainy days) for the year so far.

See daily weather forecasts

Maps App

The Maps app is a fun, functional, and fascinating app that helps you find your way to new places. You can choose from a road view or an aerial view style; you can add traffic flow; you can move quickly to your current location; and you can easily map directions from one point to another. You can zoom in and out from micro to macro with a pinch gesture or by clicking the – and + controls along the left side of the Maps window.

And because this is a Bing app and it's allowed to use your location in searches, the Maps app can display additional information about the area you're searching—find restaurants, hotels, entertainment, and more—all with a simple and free app. Nice.

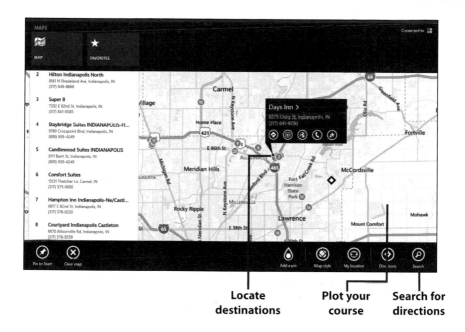

Locate destinations   **Plot your course**   **Search for directions**

News App

The News app aggregates news stories from top news sources to give you national and world news on the topics that interest you most. You can personalize the app using the My News feature to bring you stories on your favorite subjects, such as politics, health, technology, and more, or you can browse the app links to find something that catches your eye. And if you have a favorite publication, you can use the Sources feature to choose specific sources in national and world news, business, technology, entertainment, politics, sports, lifestyle, science, music, gaming, and regional news.

Once again, in the News app, you get benefit of the amazing Bing photos available through the Bing search app as well as other Bing-related apps. When you swipe up on the News app screen, instead of seeing options appear in the apps bar at the bottom of the page, you get tabs at the top, similar to what you'd see in Internet Explorer 11.

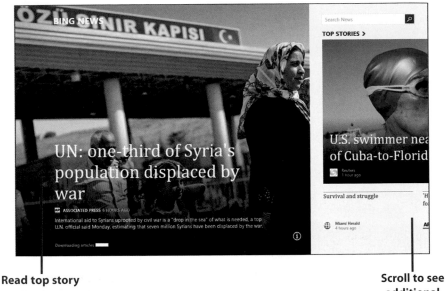

Read top story

Scroll to see additional breaking news

Sports App

The Bing sports app caters to sports fans of all types. When you tap or click the app tile on the Start screen, you see a compelling photo related to the major sports story of the moment. You can click or tap the title to display the full article. Scroll to the right to see additional top news stories, check schedules of your favorite teams, and browse recent magazine articles from your favorite sports sources.

You can personalize the app to track your favorite teams by swiping up or down on the screen and choosing Favorite Teams. You can also choose options related to different sporting areas or see what the best of the Web has to offer in the sporting world.

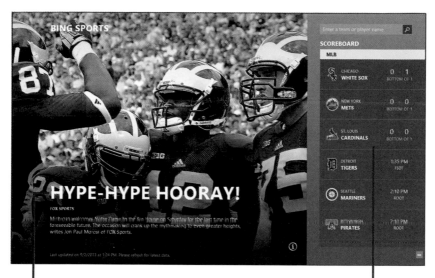

Read top story

Get information on
your favorite teams

Travel App

Because of Bing's beautiful photos, the Travel app is particularly compelling, inviting you to daydream a little while you do your daily work. When you tap or click the Bing Travel tile, the Bing Travel screen appears, with a lovely image to pull you in. You can tap or click on the information icon to find out more about the spot featured in the photo.

You can scroll through what the app has to offer by swiping to the left. You'll first see a grid of photos from whatever the featured destinations happen to be. Swipe up from the bottom or down from the top or right-click. Your Travel options appear at the top of the screen. You can choose to plot a destination, find a flight, look for lodging, or search online for more information and arrangements. Even though the Travel app offers a lot of inspiration, it's a practical tool too, helping you compare prices, find flights, and use filters to make your arrangements and find the features you need in your price range.

Continue to the right and you'll see panoramas, which are 360° images of a famous travel destination, like Paris, France; Barcelona, Spain; or New York, New York. To view a panorama, tap the tile you want to use and use your finger or your mouse pointer to move the image in a full circle. It really does feel like the next best thing to being there.

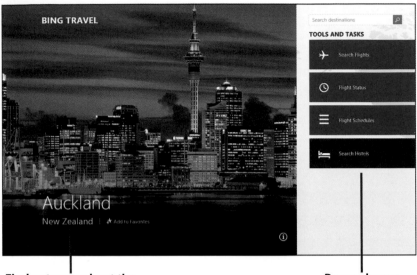

Find out more about the
displayed destination

Research your
travel plans

The Windows Store Revisited

The Windows Store has been redesigned in Windows 8.1. Now you'll get more information on the screen about various apps and be able to find the information you need to decide whether an app is right for you.

You'll find all kinds of apps there, both from Microsoft and from a world-full of developers who have been working on producing apps since the original release of Windows 8 was little more than a gleam in developers' eyes. You'll find many free apps and many apps you purchase, along with a robust user community that actively comments and recommends (or not) the apps they discover.

You launch the Windows Store by clicking or tapping the Store app tile on your Start screen. The Windows Store opens and displays a rotating presentation of top apps in the store. You can then look through the apps by category, browse through apps, or search specifically for the app you want.

Using App Categories

You display the app categories in the Windows Store by swiping down on the top of the Store screen or by right-clicking the page. The Windows Store organizes the multitude of apps into the following 20 categories:

Games	Lifestyle
Social	Shopping
Entertainment	Travel
Photo	Finance
Music & Video	Productivity
Sports	Tools
Books & Reference	Security
News & Weather	Business
Health & Fitness	Education
Food & Dining	Government

To display apps in a particular category, simply tap or click that category. The resulting apps are displayed in the Windows Store in the following subcategories:

- Popular Now
- New Releases
- Top Paid
- Top Free
- See All

You can also search for a specific app within that category by entering the phrase or title in the Search for Apps box in the upper-right corner of the screen.

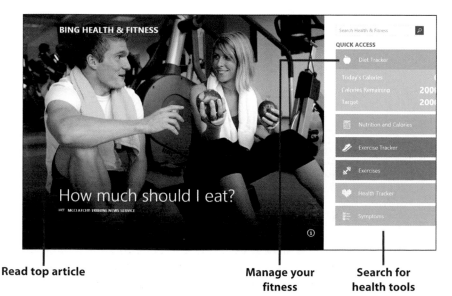

Read top article   **Manage your fitness**   **Search for health tools**

Browsing Apps

If you're interested in wandering the aisles of the Windows Store or looking to discover something new, you can swipe your way through the various categories and tap or click into tiles that seem to hold promise.

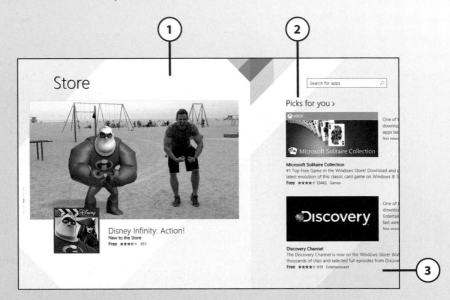

1. Display the Store by tapping the Store tile on the Start screen.

2. Scroll to the right to browse through all the app categories.

3. Tap or click an app category to display and browse through all apps in that category.

Keeping Ratings in Context

If you sort the results by the highest user ratings, be sure to check out the number of ratings that have been entered. If the app you're considering has 5 stars, that's great, but if only 2 people have entered ratings, that isn't as big a testimony as an app that has only 4 stars but has been reviewed by 75 people.

Getting App Info

When you tap the tile of an app you're interested in, the app information is displayed full-screen so you can find out more about the app and decide whether you want to download it. Each app shows you the user ratings for the app so far; displays the price (free apps say "Free"); gives you an Install button; displays the permissions the app requires; and tells you the size, category, publisher, and age rating for the app.

Swiping or scrolling to the right takes you to the Details screen, where you can read additional information about the displayed app. This might include any release notes the app publisher provides, the type of processors the app supports, and the various languages in which the app is available. Note that the information on the Details page will vary from app to app, and not all app publishers offer similar information about every app. Begin by tapping an app you want to learn more about. The screen for that app appears.

Price of app   **Check ratings**

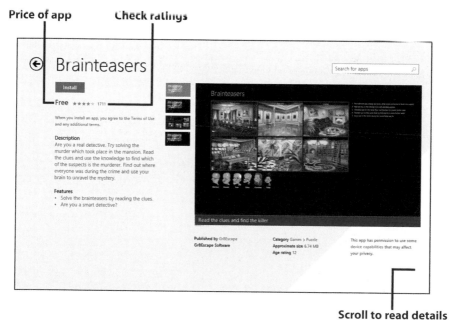

**Scroll to read details
and user reviews**

Reading App Reviews

Depending on the popularity of the app you're viewing, you might find a huge number of online reviews for the app that can help you make a choice about whether to install it on your computer. The Reviews feature is well developed, showing you at a glance how each user who posted a review rated the app, when the review was posted, and whether or not others found that particular review helpful. All this is good information to help you determine if this is the app for you.

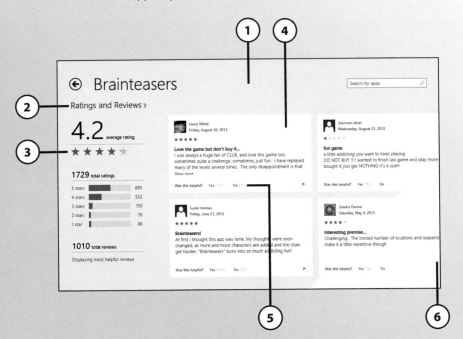

1. Display the app you want to view.

2. Scroll to the right to see the Ratings and Reviews area.

3. Check out the user ratings.

4. Read the reviews posted.

5. Indicate, if you wish, whether you found the review helpful.

6. Scroll to see more reviews.

Installing Apps

When you've found an app you like and decide to install it, the how-to is simple: Tap or click Install. Windows displays a small notification in the upper-right corner of your Store screen, and when the app is finished installing, you'll see a larger notification. Unless you've turned off sound notifications, you'll also hear a little chime indicating that the install is complete.

You can then press the Windows key or tap Start in the Charms bar to return to the Start screen and find your new app. It will appear on the far-right side of the Start screen, so swipe left, find the app tile, and tap or click it.

App is ready for use

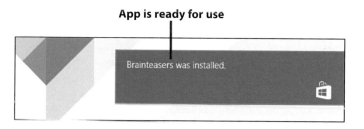

Brainteasers was installed.

Viewing Your Apps

Apps are so easy to install that in a short period of time you can forget which ones you've installed on your computer. Luckily, Windows keeps track for you.

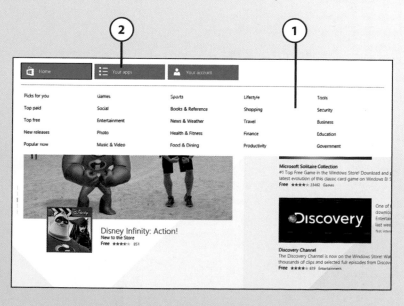

1. Display the Windows Store and either swipe down from the top of the screen or right-click the mouse.

2. Tap or click Your Apps.

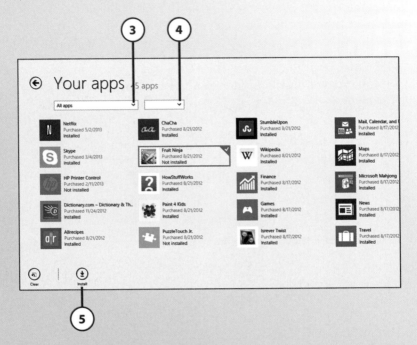

3. Click the arrow to choose which apps you want to view (apps you have downloaded but not installed or apps you've installed).

4. If you like, sort your apps by date instead of name. (By name is the default sort order.)

5. If you haven't yet installed an app and want to install it now, select the app and tap or click Install.

Adding Your Own Review

After you've used the app a little while, you might want to return to the Windows Store and add your own review that gives others the benefit of your experience. You'll notice when you return to the app in the Windows Store that there is now a Write a Review link just above and to the right of the app rating.

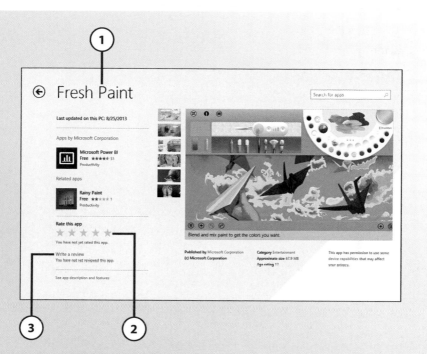

1. Display Your Apps as explained in the previous section, and select the app you want to review.

2. Click the number of stars you want to assign to the app.

3. Click or tap Write a Review.

4. Type a title for your review.

5. Type the review you want to post. (The limit is 1,000 characters, so be brief.)

6. Tap or click Submit to save your review.

Oh, What I Meant to Say

If, after you submit your review, you think of something you meant to include—or something you wish you hadn't included—you can make changes by tapping or clicking Update Your Review in the app details screen. Your review will appear in the edit window, and you can make any changes you'd like to make. Click or tap Submit when you're happy with the review and want to post it.

Purchasing an App

The process of locating an app is the same, whether the app is a free app or one you need to purchase. You'll see the cost of the app in the small app tile that appears as you search or browse, and when you open the app details screen for that app, the price of the app appears just below the rating stars. When you want to purchase an app, you begin the process by tapping or clicking the Buy button.

1. With the app screen displayed in the Store window, tap or click Buy.

2. The Buy button changes to a Confirm button. To complete the sale, tap or click Confirm.

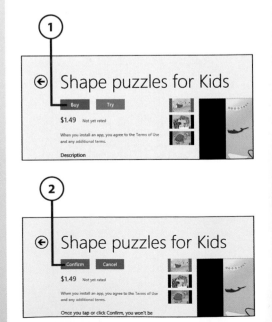

Well, Not Exactly

The Windows Store warns you that you won't be able to cancel the action after you choose Confirm, which isn't exactly accurate because on the next screen when you are asked to enter your Microsoft account login information, you can click Cancel if you change your mind.

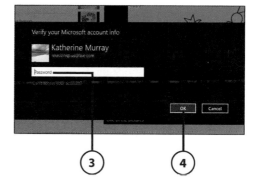

3. When prompted, type your Microsoft account password.

4. Click OK. The app is purchased using your Microsoft account and is installed on your computer.

HOW DID THEY KNOW THAT?

>>>Go Further

You might be surprised that the Windows Store can complete the purchase without any further action from you. How did it know how to charge you?

If you've purchased anything through Xbox or have an Xbox Live account or Zune music pass (now Xbox Music Pass), Microsoft has your credit card number on file, unless you specified otherwise. So, don't panic if the info shows up. It's actually kind of nice to know you don't have to go searching for your wallet. And it also makes it w-a-a-a-a-y too easy to buy Microsoft Points when you find a game you like or a movie you want to watch in the Video app, which is probably the idea. Good one, Microsoft.

Index

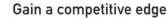

MAKE THE MOST OF YOUR SMARTPHONE, TABLET, COMPUTER, AND MORE!

ISBN 13: 9780789751577   ISBN 13: 9780789750754   ISBN 13: 9780789750334   ISBN 13: 9780789748539

Full-Color, Step-by-Step Guides

The "My..." series is a visually rich, task-based series to help you get up and running with your new device and technology and tap into some of the hidden, or less obvious features. The organized, task-based format allows you to quickly and easily find exactly the task you want to accomplish, and then shows you how to achieve it with minimal text and plenty of visual cues.

Visit quepublishing.com/mybooks to learn more about the My... book series from Que.

My Windows 8.1

Katherine Murray

que

Safari
Books Online

FREE
Online Edition

Your purchase of *My Windows 8.1* includes access to a free online edition for 45 days through the **Safari Books Online** subscription service. Nearly every Que book is available online through **Safari Books Online**, along with thousands of books and videos from publishers such as Addison-Wesley Professional, Cisco Press, Exam Cram, IBM Press, O'Reilly Media, Prentice Hall, Sams, and VMware Press.

Safari Books Online is a digital library providing searchable, on-demand access to thousands of technology, digital media, and professional development books and videos from leading publishers. With one monthly or yearly subscription price, you get unlimited access to learning tools and information on topics including mobile app and software development, tips and tricks on using your favorite gadgets, networking, project management, graphic design, and much more.

Activate your FREE Online Edition at
informit.com/safarifree

STEP 1:   Enter the coupon code: BRYFXBI.

STEP 2:   New Safari users, complete the brief registration form.
Safari subscribers, just log in.

If you have difficulty registering on Safari or accessing the online edition,
please e-mail customer-service@safaribooksonline.com